I0560140

MOLDING MINDS

A Blueprint to Forge Your Greatest Path

JOHN GRDINA WITH RYAN EUBANK

MOLDING MINDS

A Blueprint to Forge Your Greatest Path

JOHN GRDINA WITH RYAN EUBANK

Printed and Electronic Versions
Hardback: 978-1-956353-52-5
Paperback: 978-1-956353-53-2
eBook: 978-1-956353-54-9
(John Grdina with Ryan Eubank/Motivation Champs)

All rights reserved.
No part of this book may be reproduced or transmitted in any form or
by any means, electronic or mechanical, including photocopying, recording,
or by any information storage and retrieval system, without permission in
writing from the copyright owner.

The book was printed
in the United States of America.

Special discount may apply on bulk quantities.
Please contact Motivation Champs Publishing to order.
www.motivationchamps.com

I have interacted with hundreds of educators from 35 countries, and few are equal to Ryan and John when it comes to passion, commitment, and results. The way they care about students magically unlocks latent abilities within young hearts, and when I personally witnessed the transformation of non-engaged students into vibrant learners, I became a believer. Even if you, too, are a gifted and effective educator, their ideas can make you even better at what you do.

— Carl Peters, Director of Global Education (retired),

The Lincoln Electric Company

As I reflect on my time as a teacher, school counselor, assistant principal, principal, and superintendent, one thing I learned that should resonate with all educators (and non-educators) is that genuine care for students will positively impact how they react and respond when faced with challenges. I would recommend reading the stories that are told in the pages of this book, as they capture the essence of what genuine care looks, sounds, and feels like. This book should serve as inspiration for anyone who is truly working toward 'Molding Minds'!

—Dr. Scott J. Hunt, Executive Director of Field Relations,

The Ohio Department of Education

This book clearly demonstrates how commitment to and compassion for others translates into building hope and direction in the lives of those who are finding their way or have become misguided. Viewing oneself as a change agent for the betterment of our youth is clearly demonstrated in the stories told within the book, demonstrating action steps educators, counselors, parents, and community members can take to affirm others and fulfill the role of mentor and coach. From this counseling professional's view, the book is inspirational, motivating, and offering concrete action steps designed to encourage a positive mental framework which we can share with youth and others we encounter in life.

— *Gail Michalski, LPC-S, LSW*

Undergraduate professors and instructors would greatly benefit from this wonderfully practical, insightful, and so relevant book. The authors combine their impressive experience and backgrounds to approach dealing with and helping students, colleagues, and even family in a very positive manner. I am a fan of this book!

— *LTC Steven Oluic, PhD, U.S. Army retired*

I had the pleasure of working with Ryan Eubank and seeing the transformation of his welding students. They do not just learn course material, but gain real world skills, become excited and confident to learn more, and recognize the opportunities this type of education creates for their careers and future. It is as if the students were waiting for a spark to be ignited so the transformation could begin. In all my years as a student and a professor I have not seen such success in the classroom. And yes, this type of teaching has similar results for other subject material, even math!

—*Rich Basinski, MSME, Professor, PE retired*

MOLDING MINDS

A Blueprint to Forge Your Greatest Path

JOHN GRDINA WITH RYAN EUBANK

Contents

Dedicated to anyone who feels helpless
and has no hope for their future.

Introduction

It was a fall day on the weekend, and I was playing backyard football when I tackled my cousin hard. After the tackle, he got up and started crying. I didn't know why he was crying, except that I might have hit him too hard. The next thing I knew, my uncle came right over to me and started to tell me that I was dumb and stupid. He went even further and said that I would never amount to anything in my life and that I would always be stupid.

My uncle's words cut me like a knife because, at this time, I felt like an outsider in school because of my disability. I felt as though the whole world was crashing down on me and that I was a good-for-nothing kind of kid. That moment in that backyard was a memory I'll never forget because it reaffirmed what I felt kids thought of me at school—"What a dumb kid."

Being separated from regular education students at an early age so I could get help with my disability had a major impact on my identity and self-confidence. I felt like an outsider, someone who was different, and someone no one wanted to be around. It was a very low point in my life; I was a sixteen-year-old for whom school was a hard battle to face each day because I learned differently than everyone else. I just wanted to fit in and not be viewed as an outcast, and the only people who did not make me feel that way were my family, my girl-friend, and my special education teachers.

-- *Ryan Eubank*

I walked into Ryan's classroom on the last day of school, and I saw this huge, strong, tough-as-nails student, Kurtis, sitting face-to-face with Ryan and crying his eyes out. As I stopped in my tracks, all I could think to myself was, who died? The emotions were that intense. Ryan had his arms on Kurtis's shoulders, and the young man's crying was uncontrollable as tears ran down his face.

I didn't want to interrupt this highly emotional scene, so I sat back and just watched and listened to the conversation. Words like 'leave me' and 'never forget you' were spoken.

As I slowly approached Kurtis and Ryan, I heard Kurtis say, "You were the only person in my life that ever gave a damn about me. You were a father to me, Mr. E, and now you are leaving."

Ryan responded, "I'll never leave you, Kurtis. Even though I'm changing schools, I will still talk to you and help you

with anything in your life."

Kurtis said that he would fail now that Ryan was leaving and no one cared about him because he, like Ryan at a younger age, felt like he was stupid and an outsider.

Ryan and I both comforted him and let him know that he was loved and that he wasn't a bad person or stupid but instead had many gifts and talents that he could use for good in this world.

We all hugged. Everyone was crying, not only Kurtis, Ryan, and myself, but other students who had come into the classroom as well to tell Mr. E that they would miss him more than ever.

As the day passed and the kids left school on their final day, I sat in the classroom with Ryan and told him that I was going to miss him and that I understood why he was leaving, because he couldn't be Ryan at the school where he was currently teaching. He was looking for a new opportunity, a school where he could use his passion for good all the time and not feel like he was in a box, checking off a list every day to comply with the standards of the educational process.

Ryan and I embraced in a huge hug, and I told him that I love him. Later that week, I wrote him a letter explaining the impact he not only had on the kids but on me as well. (See Appendix A to read the letter.)

Ryan was different, unique, and special in a good way. I never met anyone in my life who had such love for others and a work ethic that never stopped. His passion for helping kids be worldwide-recognized welders was boiling in his blood every waking moment because he knew the pain he had felt when he was a little kid at school. He didn't want kids to suffer in school like he had; instead, he wanted to give them hope that they could be the best welder, technician, manufacturer, or whatever job they chose—because they weren't stupid or dumb.

Many kids who came to the welding lab chose it because it was a non-traditional path to make money and have a career. Ryan knew this, and as a result, he wanted each person who set foot in his classroom to feel accepted and to understand that learning differently was something that should be embraced instead of looked down upon.

In each kid who entered his room, Ryan saw a resemblance to his younger self, a low-confidence learner who just wanted to be loved and accepted.

Ryan looks at each child as his own and wants the best for them. He truly and literally would give them the clothes off his back, boots off his feet, and cars that he owned (four of them) if it meant that his students would have an opportunity to succeed. Ryan knows that his fulfillment in life is based on molding his students' thinking so they do not feel stupid but instead feel confident in their ability to make a great life for themselves and their future in any career they choose.

This book is a compilation of stories about Ryan's love for

all of those around him and the impact that he has had, is having, and will have for generations to come.

My hope is that when you read each chapter, something resonates in your heart and lights a fire to start living the life that you were meant to live and to never feel doubt or stupidity for being different or being looked at differently by your family, school, or society. There is greatness within you. All you must do is take action and let the world see it!

APPENDIX A

June 5th, 2008

Dear Ryan,

It has been one hell of a ride with you, my friend, from the days of you coming down to my old room and having 'shin-kicking' contests and joking around with your students today. Your makeup as a person has not changed since I first met you. I didn't know what to think of you at first, Ryan. I'll be honest, I thought that you were a loud, fat, funny guy who had the best rooster call I've ever heard! The past three years, you haven't altered who you are, and I think that is amazing.

Working with you this past year made me realize what an amazing person you are and how you have changed so many lives. Observing your lectures and interactions with the students in the class as well as the lab, your goal is clear as a teacher, YOU WANT THE BEST FOR YOUR STUDENTS. Your teaching philosophy is what every teacher and school should emulate because that is why we became teachers in the first place. Ryan, you have changed so many lives and always want the best for your students, but it goes further than that. You are selfless, you care so deeply for your students that you go above and beyond to make time for them, listen to them, and help them succeed in their lives by finding out what goals and aspirations they have as individuals. You treat each of your students with respect and think of each of them as equals. You do not judge, since learning from your own experience that judging people does not do anything but block you from seeing the true person beneath the surface of who they are.

For example, with Kurtis this year, you were told that he was a bad kid and that he would give you problems. In the beginning of the year, he did just that, but you did not give up on him since you knew that there was more to him than just the tough guy and a druggy. You saw that he had potential to do anything that he wanted if he only believed that he could. He couldn't believe in himself because the fact of the matter is you have to have someone believe in you first before that can happen. He would have never believed in himself if it wasn't for you giving him a second chance and being behind him 100% to make him realize that he was a good welder and that he could be somebody much more than he saw himself.

Today, when you called me down to witness the heart-break of Kurtis and the bond that you two created that would soon be gone next year because of you leaving, it was a sight I will never forget. Watching you two together, embracing each other and talking about the importance of values and family was remarkable. I don't think that you will see many teachers have such a strong connection with students as you do with yours.

Personally, you have made me a better person and have changed my life.

Knowing you has made me look deeper at my purpose in life and what I can offer to other teachers as well as to students. I know that you believe in me and that someday I may be a supervisor, principal, or superintendent. You were the first person to actually believe that I could be in a position of that caliber, and I know that in the near future, I will be—and it began with a spark from you. Besides believing in me, you and I together when we work "always turn anything we do into gold." The reason that we do this is that we respect each other's opinions and have a great work ethic. Even though we did not get much or any credit for things that we created (mini bike, gate, and other projects), I know that my experience at school with you wouldn't have been the same if it wasn't for working alongside you. I know that we wanted to do even more while at Auburn but were not permitted; but if we could have, I know the result would have been out of this world!

Ryan, you truly are a loving and caring individual, and with the right support at your next school, I know the skies are the limit for you. I know that when somebody has confidence in you and believes in you, things once thought impossible become possible. I want to leave you with a quote about changes in one's life; thought it would be appropriate for our situation. "I refuse to go backward. I am going forward with God. I'm going to be the person He wants me to be. I'm going to fulfill my destiny." Ryan, go forward and let the world know that you are here and change as many lives as you can because kids need you in their lives; they just don't know it yet. I love you, buddy.

Sincerely,

John C. Grdina

CHAPTER 1

—

Little Dummy

Someone was in the hallway, crowing like a rooster. This noise was literally like hearing a rooster from a farm in the school. It wasn't just once either, the noise of **COCK-A-DOODLE-DOO** echoed throughout the building. I went out to see which student was making such a boisterous sound—**and it was the welding teacher!**

Ryan introduced himself and told me that he recently came from the Lincoln Electric welding school as an instructor. He also explained that this is the first time that he was teaching high school students. During our conversation, he just exuded confidence and energy.

Have you ever met someone in your life who makes you step back and think, *how can that person be so happy and see the good in people all the time?* Ryan was and is that person. His attitude is the epitome of a positive outlook on life. I was drawn in by his personality. I didn't see his learning disability at first. Many people learn to mask dyslexia, keeping it hidden from others.

In the first year we met and worked together, we built a strong relationship. During the time we worked together, as the special education teacher for his classroom, he started to ask me to type his lesson plans for him. He wasn't asking me to create the lesson plans; he only wanted me to type them as he spoke them to me. I was a little taken aback by the request.

"Why don't you do it yourself?" I asked.

"I have dyslexia," he told me. "I struggle to write what I mean to say. But if you don't mind helping me, it would mean the world to me."

So, we worked together on his lesson plans. He spoke them; I typed. One day, he interrupted what he was saying to ask, "How in the world do you do that?"

"Do what?" I asked.

"Type, without even looking at the keyboard." It was mind-blowing to him.

"I did so much of this in college; it's almost second nature," I said. I hardly had to think about what my fingers were doing, much less look at them.

"I would *die* to be able to do that," Ryan said. "I use one finger, one jab at a time."

That's when I began to understand that the life of Ryan Eubank is a marvel much greater than my typing.

Many people give up on their goals and dreams. They never accomplish their goals and let their dreams slide away because they think and say, "I can't do it." Through the years, Ryan had been told he couldn't do things and he'd never amount to anything because of his disability. But as of this writing, he's been a career and technical teacher for the past nineteen years, doing what everybody, except a select few people, thought was totally beyond the reach of a boy with severe dyslexia.

Ryan has used his experiences as a student with a learning disability to benefit his personal life and his professional life. That's right. Benefit. His years as a student who struggled with reading and writing taught him to work harder than others. Those experiences gave him, as an educator, the ability to better connect with students and their discomforts. **Memories of being told he couldn't achieve are what now drive him to help his students persevere and achieve extraordinary outcomes.**

As a result of his own experience, he knows that many of his students feel as though no one believes in them. Some educators give up on difficult students, saying, "They won't amount to anything." When Ryan's students tell him about negative comments other teachers have made to them in the past, it lights a fire in his belly to help them strive to push themselves and prove those people wrong. Some students may think they can't be helped because they can't do a math problem, or they can't write an essay, or they can't read the chapter and answer the questions at the end of the chapter. When they come to Ryan's class, he can show them how to do those math problems utilizing their hands, how to intelligently hold a conversation, how to interview for a job, how to get a job, and how to become successful upon completing high school. He's been able to help his students achieve goals that everybody else thought would be impossible.

"I'm here to help my students rewrite their story," Ryan said.

After high school, his students will be able to take care of themselves by getting paid for a good job. **That's what it's all about. Rewriting stories.**

THE HISTORY OF RYAN EUBANK

As Ryan was growing up, his greatest teachers were his parents. They were patient, understood him, and showed compassion during his frustrations at school. While Ryan tried to navigate through school and life, they learned to show love and support for him when many others were not willing to do so. His family was and is the foundation he leans on. Support and love are the characteristics that not only Ryan needed, but all of us need as well.

Ryan's story begins in second grade when he went to Hale

Road Elementary, and the school was trying to figure out if he had ADHD or dyslexia. The diagnosis was dyslexia, a learning disorder marked by an impairment of the ability to recognize and comprehend written words. Here he also met Linda Clayton, who was his special ed teacher. During this period in his life, he learned to become a great teacher because of Mrs. Clayton.

Ryan recalls, "I would watch her teach a small group of students, and she would work her way around the room, teaching in different ways for each student's needs. She was kind and compassionate and knew how to interact with the students to help them gain confidence in each subject they were learning. Mrs. Clayton was a superhero, and once I began teaching, I wanted to practice those same tactics with my students."

Throughout Ryan's school years, he was put into special classes called Learning Disabled (LD) classes, setting apart those who had learning disabilities from 'regular education' students. In elementary school, learning disability was a label you wore during the school day because you would leave the regular ed. classroom. Ryan attended Mrs. Clayton's class from second grade until fifth grade. Once sixth grade started, he assimilated back into the regular education classroom.

Even though his environment was in the regular education classroom, he still had special education services provided, since he was on an I.E.P (Individualized Education Program). By federal law, students with a disability will have direct services for the specific area of their disability. Ryan went to special ed. classes for his reading disability or for extra time on assignments. He also received special tutoring and speech therapy because of a speech impediment, tongue thrust. During his regular education class, he would be called out of class by his special ed. teacher to work on his weaknesses as a learning-disabled student. This put the spotlight on him and made matters worse, and he started to feel very uncomfortable and stupid during this time in his life.

Observing everyone else, Ryan saw that learning was easy for most other kids. But he had a disability that was invisible to most people. When the regular education kids saw him or others struggling with reading and writing, the words 'Little dummies!' rang in his ears. It may not have been every day, but Ryan could see it and hear it from afar.

His spirit was crushed almost every day.

Having been a pretty good athlete, he was able to fit in better with the regular education students than some of his LD classmates; most of them had a harder time socializing since they didn't have the same athleticism he had, and they were often left on the sidelines, alone and picked on. Ryan was taken aback as he listened to his teammates talking about his friends in the LD classes; it really tore him up to see those kids being picked on or left out—because he knew that 'those kids' were the most amazing kids.

What was routine for other students required extra effort from Ryan. For example, teachers would say, "All right, go home and read Chapter Six and answer the questions in the back of the book." Regular ed. students might take fifteen to twenty minutes to do that assignment, but an individual with a disability—like Ryan—would need hours to complete this. So, what would happen? He'd bring this anxiety home to his parents and siblings.

School, however, had been easy for them, and because of that, they didn't understand what their son was going through. Eventually, he avoided asking them for help. As the school years progressed, they would ask him if he had any homework, any unfinished assignments, and he would say no—even when he did have work to be done. He didn't want to ask for help because he didn't want to put all that weight on his parents; he knew they had other obligations going on with work and with his siblings, and he didn't want to add more stress to their life. At the end of the quarter, they'd ask why he was failing or had a bad grade. Inevitably, Ryan's parents figured out that he wasn't doing his homework and not performing well on tests. This cycle lasted throughout all of his school years.

Ryan got through school with help from specific teachers, Tami Shipman being one of them, who helped him after school. He also had family, friends, and girlfriend at the time, Heather, who has been his wife for twenty-six years now.

"If it wasn't for people who loved and supported me during school, I would have dropped out because it was too hard."

Ryan knew he was different because he couldn't learn like the 'regular' students, but he watched and observed amazing special ed. teachers, who differentiated instruction to help him become a better learner. When he began teaching, he related everything back to his experiences as a student and how difficult it was for him to learn. His passion as a teacher for making sure his students understand how to become a great welder by learning the concepts is what drives him daily because, as long as he lives, he never wants one student to feel left out or feel like a 'little dummy.'

RYAN'S RULES:

1. Put yourself in other peoples' shoes before you make a comment.

2. Ask for help, especially if you feel like you are drowning in your education.

3. You can use your scars as steppingstones to your future success.

4. Find a good mentor!

Applied knowledge + Changed behavior = Transformation

CHAPTER 2

Connecting

Ryan has a natural way of making instant connections. With his vibrant and outgoing personality and the energy he brings to everything he does, he has made strong connections with students in his twenty-plus years as an educator. He's been able to do this because of his loving heart and genuine concern for each student's well-being. This cannot be more vividly illustrated than through the story of a former pupil.

Craig was in Ryan's first-ever welding class at Auburn Career Center, and boy did he know how to ruffle Ryan's feathers.

One rainy fall afternoon, Ryan and I were sitting in the cafeteria when we saw a group of kids staring out the windows. We went over to see what the rise was all about, and we saw Craig standing on a ledge and dancing in the rain while people ran in and out of the building, giving him dollar bills.

Ryan immediately went outside, prompting Craig to get

inside and to Ryan's office.

Ryan asked Craig why he was acting so foolishly outside in the rain in front of the entire school, and the student replied that he was couch surfing at a friend's house and needed money for food.

"Why didn't you tell me, buddy? I would have given you some money," said Ryan.

As their conversation progressed, they eventually made a phone call to Craig's mom. That phone call between the three of them resulted in Craig being allowed to go back home, have meals each day, and sleep in a warm bed.

Ryan furthered the conversation, asking Craig what he thought his purpose in life might be and what he wanted to do after high school. Craig had no answers, so Ryan suggested the military. Craig needed discipline in his life, Ryan explained, and serving the country would be an honorable duty.

The next day rolled around, and Craig came to school all excited. He told Ryan that after their conversation, he had ridden his bike ten miles to the recruiter's office and enlisted in the US Navy.

"You did what?" Ryan exclaimed. "I didn't mean to sign up right now. I meant, investigate it, and if it makes sense, go ahead and do it—**after you graduate.**"

"Well, if you thought it was good for me to do this, I trusted your advice, Mr. E," Craig replied.

The fact that Ryan *cared* had impacted Craig so powerfully that he made a huge pivot in his life.

He went to basic training immediately after high school. During basic training, he, like everyone else, was administered a physical. Doctors found that he had a heart condition, and the military went forward with a corrective procedure and operated on Craig. After surgery, the doctors told Craig that the benefits of this corrective surgery would last only ten years. He was honorably discharged and took one day at a time as a welder for local businesses. He worked hard and lived a simple life and later met a young lady, and they had a baby boy.

During his twenties, Craig continued to communicate with Ryan, especially each Father's Day, where he would be the first to call him—until the day Craig didn't wake up. This day came exactly ten years after his surgery for the heart condition.

Ryan, his former students, family members, and friends attended the funeral. They passed out wristbands imprinted with Craig's full name, and Ryan still wears his to this day. It's a reminder to Ryan and to all of us that life is short and precious.

Time goes by so quickly, and we all—teachers, parents,

friends, and family members—need to make the most of our time with the people we see daily, those we talk with occasionally, and even those we are meeting for the first time. **Caring connections will help all of us be more present, more authentic, and more influential in others' lives.**

QUALITY TIME CAN CHANGE LIVES

Early one October morning in 2020, Ryan was walking with his students in a metro park. That morning, a young lady was talking with Ryan about her past and how she was raised. Ryan knew her mother had been a big part of her life, but on this day, he asked her how often she saw her dad. He was taken aback by her answer.

"My dad committed suicide when I was only a couple months old," the girl told him. She followed up with, "You're the father figure in my life."

At that moment, Ryan knew that being with his students and truly getting to know them made all the difference—in both his life and in the lives of all the students he influences daily. The walks in the morning and the late nights of teaching give him extra time to season the lives of those he's in contact with. It's bigger than just welding.

 **It's about building long-lasting relationships, giving people hope through conversation, and allowing them to believe in themselves.**

As a teacher, coach, and parent, I know that each person I meet in these areas of my life needs love and support, and I don't want to neglect any of them. Therefore, being present with people, connecting with them, and being there for them is extremely valuable.

Everyone we meet in our lives has a different story, from the environment they were nurtured or not nurtured in to having healthy or unhealthy relationships they are or were in. Many people have heavy mental baggage and don't know who or where to turn to release this heaviness and enjoy the freedom of peace, love, and joy.

That's when we need people like Ryan in our lives. A mentor who is passionate about not only his craft but also about the lives of those he meets. Someone who is infectious about growing people to become the best version of themselves.

Maybe you need a person like this in your life. Do you have a mentor? Who is helping you get out of the deep mental valley you are in?

People are out there to help; you just need to take one small action to meet them. It could be through social media, or by dropping someone a DM, or by taking a class that interests you and then connecting with that teacher like Ryan, who just loves what they do and wants to help you be the best of the best, a warrior in the arena of life.

One of the greatest speeches in history regarding being an individual in the arena of life was by Theodore Roosevelt:

It is not the critic who counts; not the man who points out how the strong man stumbles, or where the doer of deeds could have done them better. The credit belongs to the man who is actually in the arena, whose face is marred by dust and sweat and blood; who strives valiantly; who errs, who comes short again and again, because there is no effort without error and shortcoming; but who does actually strive to do the deeds; who knows great enthusiasms, the great devotions; who spends himself in a worthy cause; who at the best knows in the end the triumph of high achievement, and who at the worst, if he fails, at least fails while daring greatly, so that his place shall never be with those cold and timid souls who neither know victory nor defeat.

Don't sit on the sidelines of life and feel sorry for your situation or the circumstances that have occurred in your life. Instead, be proactive by taking small steps toward your future, the future where you have hope and relate to strong, smart, and beautiful individuals who want you to blossom into the creative person that you were meant to be.

So, what do you say? Start today to get connected with someone, and if you can't find anyone, reach out to Ryan or me. We would love to be the ray of sunshine to give you hope in your life.

RYAN'S RULES:

1. Time is precious, so make the most of it in connecting and caring about the people in your life.

2. Take time out of your day to listen and build someone else up.

3. Ask people questions about themselves to find out who they truly are.

4. Remember, the more you show that you care for others, the more they will work and grow for you.

5. Stop thinking only as a leader, mentor, or teacher. Care about those you lead as *people*.

Applied knowledge + Changed behavior = Transformation

CHAPTER 3

From Poor to Rich

Ryan's story illustrates what a dramatic difference attitude can make in life. His positive attitude carried him through the challenges of dyslexia and being labeled a special education student. His family was very loving and supportive, but the real world offered little love and support to him as a kid who had trouble reading and writing. When a teacher once told him he was "not worth a damn," he didn't accept that. He was always out to prove that he was worth something and that he was born for a purpose.

Early in his high school years, he was dead set on joining the military. Then he had an accident while rock climbing at the Kissing Camels rocks in the Garden of the Gods, Colorado. He slipped and fell, breaking his wrist and forearm. Those injuries dashed his dreams of joining the military. He was upset, but his determination to succeed propelled him toward another path to become someone who would help others.

Ryan had to pivot toward his future goal and decided to

work at a local business where he could use his strengths of hand-eye coordination and building. He was hired at Lincoln Electric shortly after high school, and he worked in a shop, making welding machines. He showed an impeccable work ethic, enthusiasm, and a great outlook on life, all of which impressed his supervisors.

He found his true calling when, after five years at Lincoln Electric, he was asked to teach others how to weld. As an instructor with the company, he began his life as an educator. Ryan's fall at Kissing Camels may have kept him from fulfilling a dream of joining the military, but it led him to something else in his life. That something else was a career where he could use all his talents—speaking, helping others, and sharing his passion for welding.

Ryan can always see the good in people, especially those who have disabilities or come from a difficult background. One story of his constant pursuit to help others succeed comes from his first years as a teacher at a career and technical school. He got to know his students well and found out that he had a student in class who happened to be one of the biggest drug dealers in the city. Ryan despises drug use; he knows its ill effects and knows that users cannot get a welding job.

Ryan also knows that students of his program who can't pass a drug test are a direct reflection of him and his program. Therefore, when he got wind that one of his students was not only a user but also a dealer, he set out to remedy the situation.

With a tactful approach, he reached out to the student and asked him to assist in a night class Ryan was teaching. This gave him time with the student away from his peers, and he began to ask the young man questions about his life and his dreams. As their connection grew, the student eventually told Ryan the truth about his drug dealing (a truth Ryan already knew) and said that he really wanted to stop selling and do something more meaningful in his life.

Ryan swore to his student that if he was committed to stop using and dealing, Ryan would work his tail off to provide an opportunity for him to outearn drug dealing and to earn it the right way—through hard work and discipline. The rewards could be endless, he assured the student.

Over the years, Ryan has taken many students like this one under his wing. His positive attitude sees possibilities in them they can't see themselves, and he's committed to helping students succeed and make something of themselves. If his students work hard, receive certifications in the field, and stay clean from drugs, Ryan promises to help them find jobs through his connection with the Boilermakers. (The International Brotherhood of Boilermakers is a diverse union representing workers throughout the United States and Canada. Their members are employed in heavy industry, shipbuilding, manufacturing, railroads, cement, mining, and related industries.)

But students' success also depends on a change in their attitude. This student, inspired by Ryan's belief in him, did change his outlook. During the remainder of his time in Ryan's classes, he worked hard. He joined a national organization, SkillsUSA, where he competed in his senior year against other students from career and technical schools. With his hard work, devotion, and Ryan's positive guidance, the student placed first in the state of Ohio and third in the nation. He received awards, scholarships, and equipment. His hard work had paid off, and when he took the test for the Boilermakers, he was accepted.

Ryan's promise came out of his mindset that always looks for and believes in the good in his students. The teacher's attitude fostered a positive attitude in the student and stimulated a commitment that helped him achieve things he had never thought possible. After graduation, the young man worked for the Boilermakers for almost ten years, making $100,000 per year. He is now a father of two boys and has a wonderful wife. He explained the importance of Ryan's intervention in his life:

> *Ryan taught me to grow up and be responsible. That was the secret sauce he had, and the way he delivered his message day in, and day out showed me he cared about me as a person and my future. He also taught me life lessons that I use today to raise my own children. I will forever be*

grateful for the mentorship he gave me at the exact time I needed it most.

RICH MINDSET

Let's learn from this story. How did this young man pivot his life from drugs and possible incarceration to making over six figures per year?

Was it his ability? His education? His high school diploma?

It was none of these. Once he changed his mindset to working toward something tangible, with someone who had the experience and knowledge of how to get there, the game changed for him. He believed that he could be a prolific welder who could make good money and start having the life that he never thought possible. Ryan had planted the seed in his mind, **but ultimately the young man had to decide to act on this vision for his life.**

Life can be whatever you want to make of it because greatness lives inside of you. It's just a matter of acting on what you believe to be true.

You can make a change as well, so what are you waiting for?

Since I'm not yet a world-renowned writer, let's take it from one of the best authors on self-development, Napoleon Hill. In his book *Think and Grow Rich*, he writes:

Somewhere in the world your place is waiting for you. Through persistence and intelligent effort, you will eventually find it. You will never be defeated in your life's purpose if you keep faith in the only person in the world who controls your destiny—yourself.

RYAN'S RULES:

1. Never forget—or ignore—the importance of attitude and its impact on individual success.

2. Set a high standard for your life and help others to live by that standard.

3. Never lose hope in a person. Make them know that you love and support them.

4. Be careful what you say and do daily; those you influence will follow your actions and attitudes.

5. Have a Rich Mindset by believing in yourself and in all that you can achieve.

Applied knowledge + Changed behavior = Transformation

CHAPTER 4

Lead by Example

"Why aren't you done cleaning up the shop?" yells the foreman. "You guys can't follow directions, you never listen, and you're lazy!"

Have you heard similar words from your teachers, parents, or bosses? We follow those we respect; therefore, we need leaders who will be in the classroom, office, or shop, in the bunker with us, helping us learn how to complete a task the right way.

As a co-teacher and observer in Ryan's classes, I noticed that he would be the one with the broom or the shop pan, picking up scraps and materials from the day's work. He'd be yelling but as a reinforcer to guide the ship to its destination. He was the captain of his domain, but he swabbed the deck while the ship was on autopilot to make sure his students knew that he would never make them do something that he wasn't willing to do himself, putting in the work and being the example of how to do it right.

A true example of this is when Ryan and I were approached

by the Agriculture instructor who asked us to build a fence for their home display at The Great Big Home and Garden Show in Cleveland, Ohio. The only caveat was that we had to have this structure built within three weeks.

I looked at Ryan and said, "Do you think we can build this with no plan and in this short period of time?"

"We can do anything together, John! We are the dream team."

"Roger that!" I agreed, and we got to work laying out thin metal strips. We had to create something out of nothing, and to do that, we had to use our imagination. We began by creating different metal patterns on the floor and coming up with some models that might work. We also had the students look at our models and add their advice on how this fence could be made the best it could be since it would be on display for thousands of people at the show.

After we created something that we thought would work—which was many curves and then smaller curves inside those bigger loop structures—we asked the Agriculture instructor to come and take a look. Would this work, and would it be a good look for his display? He was shelled shocked as he walked into the welding lab. He couldn't believe we had built the design. He absolutely loved it, and we told him that we would have the entire fence built in six-foot sections, with drilled holes to connect the sections with bolts. And it would be painted black.

After the approval of the Agriculture instructor, Ryan called the class in and explained that there would be an elite team to help make this fence project a reality. He carefully chose a couple of students to help bend the metal as I guided them through the process. Another team on the ground would assemble the pieces. The welding team would tack the metal together, and a fourth team would clean up the welds using a cut-off wheel and then brushes. After the teams were assembled, we went to work.

Teamwork was a new experience for most of these students. Most of them had never even been part of an athletic team. But as I helped with the project, I witnessed a group of individuals who worked together with efficiency, execution, and communication. This project was their first opportunity to truly feel the connection in teamwork, everyone working toward a common goal. They also had an educational experience unlike any they'd ever had before, with support and instruction from a teacher who wasn't just teaching from a book, saying "Learn this," and then giving a test on material. Ryan was the glue—or in this case, the weld—that held everyone together. They worked until the bell rang each day and never complained. They loved being there, being a vital part of the production.

As this teamwork to complete the fence went on for the next couple of weeks, I looked at Ryan and said, "I honestly thought this was too big a goal to accomplish in the time we were given."

Ryan had not had any doubt. He responded that he believed so much in all of us that he knew it could be done.

After the completion of the fence, painted black and then assembled, the whole class came together and were in awe of what we had produced. Ryan and I gave everyone hugs or high-fives for their accomplishment of this great endeavor. The instructor came the next day to pick up the finished fence, and he thanked all of us and said this piece was the icing on the cake for his display.

Ryan and I, along with some of the students, went to visit the display that weekend, and we couldn't believe the final product. The black shimmered as the lights hit the fence from different angles, and our creation truly made the entire home and garden display look like a diamond on top of a hill. Many people who went through the display throughout the weekend couldn't believe that students had built this and had done it so professionally.

This great accomplishment came to fruition because Ryan was the leader. He was the master commander and led everyone by example. He believed in every single person and showed everyone how to be an important piece of the puzzle for production. Ryan is a catalyst of hope even when others think that it's not possible. **His strong belief**

in others achieving great things is truly infectious. Being around his energy makes you a better human being.

 **People in leadership must lead by simply showing up and setting an example.**

Service through love and by love, and wanting the best for others, not themselves, is what it is all about. That's why it's called servant leadership.

If I'm serving myself, how much money can I make? How much can you do for me? It's all about me, me. That's the ego. But if I have an opportunity to truly be a servant leader, I want the next generation and the generation after that to be built up. Why is this so important? Because our families, community, and nation need more leaders so our country can be restored.

Restored to what? Restored to the simplistic roots of service, love, and charity. **You are the agent of change that can influence so many people; all you need to do is get outside your comfort zone and start simply by doing the little things right.**

There are no excuses; just love, hard work, and true care for helping others. So, start today by building yourself up to be the leader so many people will need for tomorrow.

RYAN'S RULES:

1. Be the captain of your ship at home and in your community.

2. Be an example by serving others with love.

3. Be a positive human magnet. Focus on being someone people want to be around.

Applied knowledge + Changed behavior = Transformation

CHAPTER 5

—

Master Shepherd

People will follow the actions and attitudes of those they respect, especially if a leader has built caring connections with them. Who we are as people, as friends, and as part of a community influences those around us daily—probably even more than the things we preach to them. That's why the principles of connections and leading by example are so important in our own lives—if we want to give hope to others, the blueprint for success is to live it ourselves.

RYAN'S TRANSFORMATIVE TEACHING

Ever since I met Ryan, I've seen him forging long-lasting relationships. He's a master shepherd who always cares for his flock and truly protects and guides them through their lives in high school and beyond. Ryan's passion is clear:

> *I want to have passion and better the kids. My end goal is going beyond the welding hood, doing something more than just welding. My profession is not just an educator*

but a life-changer.

If it wasn't for Ryan's influence and his love for his students, many of them would now be out in the world of work, having to endure below-average jobs and 'just getting by.' Instead, in his relentless persistence to see others prosper, he has nurtured students who are now successful business owners, engineers, SpaceX employees, and great contributors to our society.

Below is a testimony from one of Ryan's former students, Logan R. He graduated from Mentor High School and Willoughby-Eastlake Technical Center in 2011.

Ryan's welding class was literally the defining moment for my life and my career. I can honestly say that without his class, I would not be where I am today. Welding was not on my mind at all as a possible career path until I visited his class in my sophomore year of high school. I'll be honest, the money welders made was my initial draw, but it quickly became more than just the money. Ryan gave me the opportunity to lead projects, to learn a skilled trade, all while providing life advice that I still use to this day. I already knew that working hard was the first step to success, but Ryan was and is living proof of that. He taught us that we need to take pride in what we do, or there's no point in doing it.

Ultimately, he's also the person who introduced me to welding engineering, a field I was completely unaware of before, which I went on to study in college and achieve my Bachelor of Science. So yeah, I wouldn't be where I am today without Ryan, and I'll be forever grateful to him for that. He's still my mentor and my teacher, but he's also a great friend. I always ask him for advice when I'm going through things about my career or if I come into some type of question about my life.

He always makes me feel comfortable when I talk to him, he is a good listener, and we never miss a beat when we talk on the phone. I started at SpaceX in March of 2021, working as a Welding Engineer on the Starship Development project in Brownsville, Texas. We have had one successful launch and we are getting ready for the second.

Ryan has provided local businesses with excellent welders, but, more importantly, he has sent them people of great character. He has built relationships that will make a difference in life.

He is also a motivator for future teachers around the country. As an educational consultant to schools and colleges, he has forged many long-lasting relationships with other teachers and instructors. The passion for his profession pours out of him as he lays down a smooth bead on that mild steel, or as the sweat beads off his brow as he does an overhead weld shirtless. Read that last sentence again. Yes, Ryan has welded above his head, shirtless, and it is a sight to see! Teachers who participate in his training classes wonder how he pulls off this 'stuff' and what else he has up his welding jacket.

Kyle Linko, a welding instructor at the Career Technology Center of Lackawanna, Pennsylvania, first met Ryan at an educators' workshop. Kyle had been to many seminars and conferences taught by people "who don't really know how to weld." (Think about that for a second—participants pay for professional development in a field, and the instructor really does not know the content?) Kyle made a connection with Ryan and now collaborates with him on a regular basis. He visits Ryan from time to time just to sharpen the blade for his craft and to pick up any tips he can on being an educator who will make a difference in people's lives as he works at developing relationships with his own students.

Kyle teaches welding, and welding is a vehicle that can take you to other places, but he knows that 'growing people' is his ultimate mission in education. He firmly believes, "If you really want to make a difference, you have to organically grow people, and it cannot be forced."

In 2006, Logan E. first met Ryan. (Yes, another Logan.) Logan's first thoughts when he met Ryan were, who is this crazy dude? What did I get myself into? Logan was sixteen, headed down a dark road, and likely to drop out of school. He had no interest in learning from a textbook, but he loved to work with his hands. Then he joined the welding class with Ryan as his instructor. Logan says:

He literally saved my life. He totally 180'd my life. He didn't care about my reputation or judge me. I dressed differently and was a burnout when I started school. Ryan usually busted my balls hard, but you knew he truly cared. He taught me the value of teamwork and how to work well with others.

Ryan's guidance set a solid foundation for Logan's life, and he got the student a job at Mitchell's Canvas and Awnings, where Logan welded and began his career in the welding industry.

After high school, Logan continued to work in the welding field, and Ryan didn't hear from him for a while. About five years later, he called Ryan at home with a welding problem. This reignited their relationship, and they began to talk more frequently. Ryan then asked Logan to help at Lakeland Community College, and there, Logan was able to help students in competitions and aided adults in getting jobs.

As their connection grew stronger, Logan began to talk to Ryan more and more about life, his relationships, and his current job. He found that Ryan was always helpful in guiding him in the right direction, even at the age of thirty. Ryan was becoming a father figure to his former student, now an adult.

One day in the fall of 2020, Logan could no longer take the stress and direction of his job and decided to change his professional career. He discovered a new passion, blacksmithing. He has goals he's working toward and the discipline to work toward them daily. He says he owes this life to Ryan's care and commitment.

Logan was even hired by Ryan at his company, Arc-Hound Welding and Fabrication, a company created in April 2020 by Ryan, his son, and former students. It's simply beautiful how Ryan has built a company with former students and his family. His teaching style has always been about building a community of teamwork, growth, and success. Now he's using that model of true relationships, creating a culture of success in his business.

When Logan told Ryan he was quitting his job, Ryan immediately asked him to come work for his new company. So, everything Ryan has poured into this young man he now has in one of his employees.

You may not be an educator, but you have influence in your relationships. All relationships impact others. Especially when we build bonds with young people, we are life-changers.

RYAN'S RULES:

1. Be available to those who seek you out.

2. Build relationships for life.

3. Let people know you will always be there for them.

Applied knowledge + Changed behavior = Transformation

CHAPTER 6

Show Up, Shut Up, and Get to Work

When I coached varsity baseball at my high school, I asked Ryan to speak with my players in one of my weekly leadership classes. I told him he could speak about whatever he wanted. He arrived, dressed in his classic steel-toe boots, jeans, flannel shirt, and sophisticated eye protectors, ready to impart words of wisdom to about twenty of my players.

He explained to the group that he was a welding instructor, and his success is measured by the performance of his welding students after they have graduated. He gave the example of one recent student who, after graduation in June, went to a national welding competition with about 40,000 other welders—and took third place. In July, he was hired for a job that by November was paying him $86,000 per year. What made him so successful?

It's simple: he shows up, shuts up, and gets to work.

It doesn't matter if you are preparing to be a master welder or a highly competitive athlete, Ryan explained, success depends on having these qualities of showing up, shutting up, and getting to work.

To have influence and be a leader in your sport, your craft, or your family, you've got to show up every day. If practice starts at 7:00 a.m., you need to be there at 6:45. You should be the one who meets and greets others. And after showing up, you have to shut up. Today many people whine and complain and make excuses for why they can't become successful at something. Get to work and do a great job every day. Then there is no skill, trade, or craft you cannot master.

Ryan also challenged the players to be themselves instead of being a 'follower.' To be great, your true self must show up and not change for anyone. "I'm Ryan Eubank," he said, "and I don't give a damn what you think of me. I know who I am. I show up every day. I will love you unconditionally, and I'll be there to change your life every day. I love my family because they let me be who I am, and they support me. What I do is not about the money; it's about the influence I have to make people's lives better."

Ryan's speech to my players was profound, and the team used his mantra of **show up, shut up, and get to work.** During that season, we took his words to heart and showed up like professionals at each practice and game. The kids took his words to heart and truly worked hard to apply these words, coupled with leadership and mindset work, to their routines in baseball, and we won our conference championship that year. I am forever grateful to Ryan for helping us to become not only better baseball players but also high-character individuals.

HOW TO TEACH WITHOUT TEACHING

Ryan's students do community service projects, and when people ask how he does it, he always replies, "I didn't do any of it. The students did it all." When people ask how he gets high school and college students alike to get things done, he says, "I teach them about life. And then as we go along with our lives, we put in a little bit of welding, and we become the best welders in the world."

It's not about welding, Ryan says. It's about all the soft skills we must teach to our community and our students. We have to show up every day on time. We've got to do what we say we're going to do, and we've got to do it well. We've got to work together as a team.

The principles of showing up, shutting up, and doing your job without whining and making excuses are the bedrock for becoming amazing workers. Those who can master these imperatives of work can be taught almost anything and will be contributors to the greater good of that business.

Ryan lives his own life in this way. He's never late; he's always on time—15, 20 minutes early—every day. He says, "If

I can show those students that I can do that, the students will do it with me. If I tell the students that I'm going to be there, I'll be there. I never want to let my students down by not being there on time, not working hard, or not showing them how to build strong work habits." When Ryan does a project with his students, he tells everybody to make sure they are there on time, and the kids will even get there twenty minutes before he does, sitting in their cars and waiting for him. They are that eager and aggressive in their desire to work with him.

Ryan also teaches new welding instructors, and he tells them to *stop* teaching welding. What? When he told me this, I couldn't believe what he was saying. "Don't teach your content, but do something else." He explained further, and it all made sense.

Ryan says if you're a machinist instructor or any type of instructor or teacher, stop teaching your craft. Stop. What you are trying to do as an educator is teach your students how to become you. And if you are not teaching them how to become you because you aren't good with yourself, and you don't feel confident in yourself, then your students won't either.

As teachers, parents, foremen, and mentors, it is our responsibility to make sure that children and adults alike understand the importance of this foundation of a great work ethic, and if we set an example through our daily actions, the younger generation will have a model to follow in doing little things the right way.

Ryan teaches his students how to show up, shut up, and do their job every day by living that work ethic himself. "If we stop teaching our craft and teach good life habits, we will become masterful at math, English, history, welding, electrical, plumbing, machining, or HVAC," he says. "We teach life, and along the way of teaching life, we add a little bit of welding and a little bit of this and a little bit of that."

When Ryan was learning welding and then became a teacher, Bill West and Joe Kolasa were his mentors. Ryan watched Bill and Joe and learned each day how they showed up early, taught with passion, and truly loved what they did. Ryan had such a high respect for his mentors that he wanted to be like them one day. In Bill and Joe, Ryan had people to look at as the exemplar, and that was how he learned what he wanted to do.

So, if you are the teacher, parent, or boss, remember that what you say and what you do has a profound impact on those around you.

If you are the student, the son, or the new employee, seek out high-character individuals you want to emulate so that you can become that person one day.

RYAN'S RULES:

1. Show up, shut up, and do a great job.

2. Success doesn't happen magically. You must put in the time and commit to being the best. It's a relentless pursuit!

3. How you model anything is how those you lead will be learning everything.

Applied knowledge + Changed behavior = Transformation

CHAPTER 7

——

Get Outside the Comfort Zone

As Ryan preaches how to do everything the right way by simply showing up, shutting up, and getting to work, his students start to adhere to these sound words. Besides this credo, Ryan also preaches about living in simplicity, using the K.I.S.S. acronym, "Keep it simple, student."

Growth toward success always starts with the basic building blocks. Becoming a great welder or living a wonderful life all starts with learning the basics of how to do something well. Ryan shares with kids that he has lived in the same house for twenty years, has driven the same truck for years, and lives for the present moment. The example of his life illustrates to students that people can have a fulfilled life without all the cars, big houses, and fancy clothes.

One student took the K.I.S.S. motto a little too far when he told Ryan, "Mr. Eubank, all I need is to make $88 a month, and I'll live under the Todd Road bridge." Corbin, Ryan's student, was brilliant, but he was *so* complacent.

Corbin had three buddies who were also in Ryan's welding class, and after school, the four of them played spoons downtown as a corner grunge band. Corbin had a personality that would light up the room, and he was an unbelievable welder and fabricator. He had so much potential, but he didn't realize how much talent he had and what he could offer to the world. Instead, he wanted to travel across the country with his band and be a nomad. He decided that if he could just make enough money to eat each day, he would be content with the bare minimum.

During Corbin's senior year in high school, he did what he wanted to do—he lived minimally and literally under a bridge. He thought that living under a bridge would give him freedom from parental scrutiny. For months, he lived like this—until two weeks after graduation. Then he saw his simple and non-linear lifestyle needed to change. Corbin called Ryan and admitted that he couldn't continue living like that. He needed a job.

Ryan had predicted that living so uncomfortably would change the young man's habits and push him to want something more. Corbin had to decide to change his lifestyle; otherwise, he'd be living in a hellacious situation, and the rest of his life could have been miserable.

His welding teacher had also known that with his abilities and skill, he would one day be an asset to a company. Unfortunately, Corbin didn't believe it until he admitted his unsatisfactory situation, planned to change it, and got moving in the right direction. This young man's life is obviously not a good illustration of the wisdom of 'keep it simple,' but his moving from effectively being homeless to now having a successful career with a company that works on nuclear reactors, submarines, and aircraft carriers for the United States Navy gives us a great example of acknowledging a situation and acting on a plan to change life for the better.

Corbin's story is a reminder to us that we should chase our dreams but also use all our talents in a way to support a solid foundation. Corbin learned that a steady income would help him get to his ultimate dream faster, which is to become well-known in his band.

Although most of us don't choose to live under a bridge and play for a grunge band, a large part of the population is content to just play the game of life … and then die. What is the 'game of life'? Get an education, get married, have kids, have a mortgage, pay off your mortgage, retire, die. Generation after generation follows the same track.

If that's the game we're playing, progress in some areas of our lives and our families' lives may happen but not at the rate it could. We're too comfortable and content. Let me say that it's not necessarily 'bad' to live a life like this. Having strong relationships at home, at work, and in the community is very important to living a purposeful life. The only question is: Are we doing just the bare minimum in these areas?

We were designed for greatness and to envision a life that is almost unimaginable. Motivational speaker Les Brown put it best:

> *The graveyard is the richest place on earth, because it is here that you will find all the hopes and dreams that were never fulfilled, the books that were never written, the songs that were never sung, the inventions that were never shared, the cures that were never discovered, all because someone was too afraid to take that first step, keep with the problem, or [stay]determined to carry out their dream.*

Don't let your dreams die! Strive to have small wins daily, build consistent habits, wake up earlier, achieve more, give more, love more, and push yourself to limits you never knew you had.

Too often, we may tell ourselves that we can't build that business or have a positive impact in our community, but **what is it that's holding you back from living a life of purpose?** Are you too comfortable to seek the desires of your heart before they end up in a graveyard?

Is there something you have a passion for, something you strongly believe in? Pursue it by using your talents. It may be scary to take a risk or believe in that dream that you have always wanted. Doubts, prior experiences, or even beliefs you hold about yourself may be the reason you are holding back from pursuing the 'future you.'

FROM FRUSTRATED STUDENT TO AMAZING TEACHER

After Ryan graduated from high school, he began working at Lincoln Electric. During this time, there were rumors that Lincoln Electric was going to move overseas, and he was worried that he might not have a job. So when Lincoln Electric offered him an opportunity to go to their welding school during the day and continue with his job at night, he took on this new avenue to keep improving his skills.

Welding school started at 8:00 in the morning and ended at 2:30 in the afternoon. Then Ryan went to work from 3:00 in the afternoon to 3:00 in the morning. Employees at Lincoln were working twelve-hour shifts because production was ramped up for the Christmas shopping season.

After he finished with work at 3:00 in the morning, he had a 43-mile drive home and then had to be back to school by 8:00 a.m., plus he had to pick up a buddy who was going to school with him. He did that for 17 weeks, never missed a day, and was always on time.

Shortly after Ryan finished the welding class, the instructors approached him with another opportunity—to become a welding instructor at Lincoln Electric.

His response was immediate and emphatic. "Absolutely not!"

Bill West, the instructor, replied, "Why not? You'd be amazing at it, Ryan. You're just the person we're looking for."

And Ryan said, "Bill, there's no way I would ever want to stand in front of a classroom and teach a class."

"But why wouldn't you want to do this?"

Ryan answered, "I don't know how to read well; I have dyslexia, and I don't like to spell."

"Those things don't matter," Bill said. "You have the skillset to do it. You've just got to do it."

A day or two passed, and another individual from Lincoln Electric came to Ryan and said, "You're going to do it. And if you don't like it, you can have your job back."

Ryan decided to give it a try and accepted the opportunity to go after this new position.

On Ryan's very first day in the classroom and within the first minute of teaching, an ironworker in the front row asked him a question. Ryan was able to rephrase the question and then answer it, so the man understood the answer. It was a life-changing moment for Ryan. Ryan said, "The man looked at me like I was a god. And at that second, right there, it was like, *I'm not an educator; I'm a life changer.* I just answered this guy that has been doing this job for 20 years. I solved his riddle in 15 seconds. I was like, wow, I can do this."

Even though Ryan had been anxious about attempting to teach, with Bill West and Joe Kolasa's mentorship, he believed he could succeed. He wanted to prove wrong all those people who thought a poor student could not possibly be a good teacher. He took on this challenge and learned everything he could in the welding arena. Including working hard to study blueprint reading, welding symbols, various welding equipment and techniques, and the science behind using welding to build structural bonds that would last a lifetime. He birthed a new, unimagined career because of two men who believed in his talents and potential—and because he was willing to embrace a very uncomfortable situation and face his fears head-on.

Because he took on this challenge to become a welding instructor, hundreds, if not thousands, of lives have been touched by the knowledge, relationships, and opportunities Ryan has provided to so many. Ultimately, welding and teaching were tools that he used to help people get jobs, make connections, and start his own business.

That risk, **that decision to do something that he thought would destroy his confidence, turned out to be the blessing that changed his life.**

RYAN'S RULES:

1. Push past fears that are holding you back from being someone with something to offer this world.

2. Start using your talents to live your purpose. Don't let your gifts and dreams pass away.

3. If someone has a vision for you or sees something in you that you don't see in yourself—believe them! It could change your life.

Applied knowledge + Changed behavior = Transformation

CHAPTER 8

Quality Time

It was a Sunday night, and I got a text message from Ryan. "Can you come walk with us tomorrow morning?"

Ryan and his students were on spring break, but my school was not. I was excited about doing this walk with him because he had invited me to come a couple of times before, and I'd never been able to go. Even though I had to work this early in the morning before the school day started, I couldn't wait to see what he had in store for the walk with his kids.

Monday morning, I woke up, said my morning prayers, grabbed my hiking shoes and headlamp, and left my house at 5:10. Driving to a local metro park where we would meet, I took a different route than usual as I thought about what the walk might be like at this time of day. This was a familiar park; I frequented it growing up, and I had just begun running the park trails with my running group on Saturday mornings. I kept imagining which route we might take once we began our journey at the famous Squire's Castle.

Squire's Castle is a historic site on the North Chagrin Reservation in Northeast Ohio. The house was built by Feargus Squire, an executive for the Standard Oil Company, at the end of the nineteenth century. Squire abandoned his plans to finish his house and sold the property to developers who later turned it into a unique historical destination for hikers and travelers. Enough about that.

I pulled into the parking lot at the castle at 5:40 a.m. and saw at least six cars with their headlights off. As many as ten to twenty students join Ryan every day for these walks in nature, for physical fitness and—maybe most importantly—to enjoy the comradery.

I chose my parking spot and turned on my headlamp to look for Ryan's red truck. When I couldn't find him or his truck, I gave him a call. He answered and said he was only a few minutes away. As he came flying into the parking lot, a flood of kids poured from the cars to meet us on the road.

Ryan introduced me to the group. That morning, three new people who didn't usually walk with Ryan had shown up. One was a former student, and the other two were a father and son duo who Ryan said had driven from Oregon to be there. What? Oregon; that's one heck of a trip for a nature walk at 5:45 in the morning. It turned out that the father had driven his son to the area for a week of Ryan's instruction on welding, and they were joining him on his morning walk.

After our introductions, I talked to the group for a few minutes about facing your fears and taking the governor off your brain—keys to living a limitless life and growing as an individual.

When Ryan told the kids that we were doing the big hill today, the look in all the kids' eyes screamed, "Oh, crap!"

"We are going to the hill!" he said, crowing like a rooster, Ryan's signature call when he's excited. His energy was infectious.

"I can't wait! It's hard, but it's worth it," said one of the students.

Then Ryan told me to turn off my headlamp and to just trust him and the group.

We trekked our way down a path at a vigorous pace. Adrenaline rushed through me. The path we were on was one I had run many times, but now, it felt like I was on foreign soil. I couldn't see more than fifteen feet in front of me, and I had to feel with my feet to detect the rocks and roots. Never in my life had I walked this type of terrain in pitch blackness. I had to calm my body, listen to what was around me, focus on staying with the pack, and strive to be where my feet were.

After getting pushed to the middle of the pack, I caught up with Ryan.

"Why no headlamps?" I asked.

"We do this to trust each other," he replied.

Man, I never would have thought of that.

As we continued our walk, I commented that the experience already was so different without my headlamp, and I didn't know where I was going. He agreed, and we talked about how these walks were different from anything his students had experienced before—and that was the magic behind them. Why would fourteen kids show up for a walk at the butt crack of dawn when they could be sleeping in?

The answer was simple. **It's the comradery and the quality of time that we spend together that makes this special.** Most other kids just wake up, check their phones, and are zombies until they eat lunch. These kids are up; they get exercise, and they work together while talking about life— all without technology. It's an experience that they long for, and no one else is showing them that the simple things in life like walking and talking can be so valuable."

We were approaching the Big Hill when we got off the trail and entered an area of dense underbrush that we had to push our way through.

"Someone find a way up this hill," Ryan said. The kids looked around for an opening in the brush.

"I found it!" one of the students yelled, and all of us

scurried over to him. The unknown of this hill became a reality, and we embarked on the adventure.

We entered an indistinct path overgrown with pricker bushes and tight branches. Pushing these aside, we forged our way through. It was still dark, and we couldn't see much, but we could see the steepness of the hill in front of us. We started up, grabbing roots for support as we climbed. At this point, I was toward the back of the pack and heard groans as the kids climbed up the hill on all fours. Some were struggling to find their footing on the path (which wasn't really a path) of mostly dirt, rocks, and roots. I was thinking it was unbelievable the kids were climbing this hill, working this hard, with no reward, compensation, or grade. At the top, Ryan and I looked back and saw a couple of students still struggling on the hill, so we went back down to give them some help and guidance. They finished the climb, and we all met at the top.

The kids were patting each other on the back and saying, "We did it!" Some, like me, had never experienced anything like this before, and the students who had done it before were still impressed that they had conquered The Hill again.

We stood at the top for a couple of minutes, watching as the sun peeked through the tree line on the eastern horizon. It was a 'Kodak memory.' From our higher elevation, we witnessed the beautiful sight of the sun beginning its climb.

The kids continued to talk about their great feat and their sense of accomplishment. The conversations all around were positive and uplifting. We congratulated each other and were excited for whatever came next.

I walked stride for stride with Ryan as we carefully traversed a steep ravine, then moved swiftly across the top of the hill to a designated walking path. This path took us back to the castle, where our cars were parked.

The experience was amazing. It was all about the time we had spent together walking, hiking, and talking. Doing it all without interruptions or distractions of technology made the event more special; I heard conversations about life, the future, and hope. Each student brought their best that morning, and it was a win for them just to show up and meet at such an early time. This also gave the experience more significance. These students chose to be there on their spring break. The relationship Ryan had built with them clearly meant even more than I had originally known.

When we finished our walk, I asked to take a picture of the group. They posed, and the flash lit up the sky and their triumphant faces.

Ryan and I each talked briefly to the group. He hammered on the point of 'embracing the suck,' and I closed it out by talking about successful people waking up early. As we spoke to the group, it was apparent that this experience and quality time would be a lasting memory, not only for me but for them as well. I know that these students will one day tell their kids about these walks and how much they loved doing something with one another that was so simple yet so meaningful.

As I drove to school that morning, I reflected on the experience. **Memories are made when we have unique experiences and do something meaningful together.** The time with Ryan and his students that morning will forever be engraved in my memory as an example of how to live life and enjoy the presence of one another.

Ryan called me later that day. We talked about our walk that morning and about our friendship, how it has grown even though we haven't worked together in the same building for over ten years, and our gratitude for the brotherhood we've developed. **People were meant to push each other to be better, and spending quality time together is part of the blueprint for the success of long-term, supportive relationships.**

Ryan devotes time beyond class to give his high school students opportunities to build their skills in welding and work on their development as people. These walks with his students, taking time out of his personal life, demonstrate his commitment to love and passion. His ability to give quality time has enabled him to build trusting and long-lasting relationships, and that is one of the biggest factors in his success as a teacher, businessman, husband, father, and friend.

Do we spend quality time with our co-workers, family members, and friends? Or do we just go through the day to survive and allow work and social media to consume our time?

 **We need meaningful relationships in our lives, and quality time is necessary to make the roots of those relationships go deep.**

Quality time allows people to learn from each other and to give hope to one another. Shared experiences and companionship like this morning hike build bonds of trust, which we all need as we strive to be the best we can be.

Imagine if we were able to take this concept into our relationships at work. Could we spend breakfast or lunch with a co-worker and get to know them better? Maybe go for a walk with a co-worker during lunch break and build each other up? We all go through trials and tribulations, and going alone only makes the light at the end seem farther away. Sometimes, we can give support by just listening. Carve time out of your day to be there for someone and be intentional as to when you are going to do this on a daily or weekly basis.

Giving people quality time seasons their lives with conversations and experiences that build hope and belief in themselves.

RYAN'S RULES:

1. Make opportunities for quality time and use the time with others to season their lives.

2. Most people won't remember you for what you taught them; they'll remember you for how you treated them.

3. Live in the present moment and be fully present with one another.

Applied knowledge + Changed behavior = Transformation

CHAPTER 9

Bird Chirp

On most mornings, I exercise in or around my house, but on April 8, 2021, I met Ryan and his students to do another nature walk at 5:40 a.m. I showed up a little early just to see if I could be the first one there. When I arrived at the trailhead parking area, two cars were already there. Again, I was amazed. *You've got to be kidding me! Two teenagers got here before me, and they aren't getting paid to be here!* (Well, neither was I.) This was the habit that Ryan had instilled in them. Remember, showing up is one of the first principles of getting hired and having a successful career.

Before we started our walk, Ryan talked to the kids about the love and commitment it takes to truly care about people and their well-being. As he was talking, a bird chirped. Ryan stopped immediately.

"Did you hear that?" he asked.

"Yes," answered some of the kids.

Ryan used this small moment to talk about something we

both believe is of crucial importance: starting your day off right.

Because we were up early, we heard that first bird chirp of the day. It was a peaceful and comforting chirp, a gentle reminder that we are a small part of this big world. Compare this to what many kids hear when they wake up—not positive words and affirmation but negative comments like "Get UP!" (shouted), "You overslept again!" "Hurry up; you have to get to school," or much worse.

What you hear and see first each morning can truly alter the course of your day. Building daily habits of waking up on time and listening to positive messages is key to starting the day off right, and starting the day off right sets the stage for you to have a positive impact in your own life and in others' lives.

Another habit that has many benefits is the habit of working hard at everything you do. Your relationships, business, and personal growth will all see positive results if this is a daily habit. Working hard simply means putting in more time with something because you want to make progress.

 **If the habit of hard work is NOT the bedrock of your daily operations, you are drifting down the river of comfort—and you'll see little to zero results.**

Remember, to do anything worth living, you must put in the work!

HARD WORK AND STRONG HABITS

John recently finished his associate degree in Applied Science in Welding and Fabrication Technology at Lakeland Community College. He graduated from Chardon High School in 2019. For an English project during his senior year at Chardon, he set out to seek more information on the process of manufacturing and then to build something himself. He connected with a foreman at Ayrshire, a local manufacturing company, who guided John in building a smoker (a grill to cook food). John wanted to build a smoker because he wanted one at home to cook food with his family. He finished the project and, in the process, discovered that he loved welding.

While John was on a visit to Lakeland Community College in the spring of his senior year, he met Ryan at the welding school. They had a conversation that lasted around three hours, and John walked away knowing that he was going to attend Lakeland to pursue a degree as a welder. Summer passed, and he began his journey as a welding student in the fall of 2019.

In high school, John played football for Chardon and developed a good work ethic while in the program. He had learned through experience that if you wanted to be successful, you had to put in the work and the time. He took these principles with him to college and applied them to become a great welder. He learned from Ryan that you must learn everything, outwork everyone, and take every opportunity to meet new people and experience new things.

Toward the end of John's first semester at Lakeland, Ryan and his assistant, Jesse Srpan, noticed John's work ethic and talent and encouraged him to take on a new role as a part-time worker at Ametco, a local manufacturing corporation. John started working there while still going to school to improve his skills as a welder.

He continued to show up, shut up, and get to work, and his next opportunity came when Ryan asked if he was interested in joining the SkillsUSA welding fabrication team. John accepted the challenge and was made team captain. This responsibility changed his life.

He already had talent and a good work ethic, but he began to build new daily habits of performance in his schoolwork, in his job, and in leading his team for SkillsUSA, often into the wee hours. He started to understand that long days and daily effort were required to make a champion, and he became a man of discipline, preparing for the SkillsUSA competition in April 2020. As all of us know, the spring of 2020 had different plans for all our lives. Like the rest of the world, John found his goals and aspirations blocked. This left a bitter taste in his mouth because he and his team had worked so hard to be ready to compete.

Time passed, and the fall of 2020 began with school and work. John hadn't given up on his goals, though. He told Ryan he wanted to be the next great champion in the welding industry. He knew Ryan had trained many great welders before, and he was excited about being 'the man.' He had an idea of the challenges ahead of him and the time and commitment it would take to be a champion. Ryan told him, "If you think you can hang with me, meet me tomorrow morning at Squire's Castle at 6:00 a.m."

John met Ryan and his high school students the following morning. The group looked as though they had been waiting for him so they could begin. He felt a sense of discomfort; it felt as though he were late, but he had been right on time. They began their walk, and he felt even more uncomfortable because he was with high school kids, he couldn't see where he was going, and at the same time, he was trying to prove to Ryan that he was 'the man.'

He thought it was crazy to be doing this. He couldn't rationalize the importance of this early morning walk. But after leaving the walk and getting to work, he noticed how different he felt. He had more energy and felt more alert than ever before in his life. He felt *amazing.*

After his day at work, he returned to Lakeland for his academic classes. He continued this new daily cycle for a couple more months and then stepped away from his full-time job so that he could commit 100 percent to being the best SkillsUSA individual competitor he could be.

John joined Ryan for the early morning nature walks and spent his days practicing his welding skills. He noticed that people looked at him differently when they knew he was gone from 5:30 a.m. until 10:00 p.m. every day. They didn't understand that he was a man on a mission—a mission to be the best welder in the nation. To do that, he put in time practice, reading, reflection, and criticism on each of his welds. **To be superior at anything in life, you must have a vision and then act on that vision while canceling all the distractions around you.** John became a man of constancy. He had learned that it takes heart to become the best at anything in this life.

He was finally able to compete at the Ohio SkillsUSA Championships in April of 2021. In the individual competition for welding, John placed first in the state.

He then advanced to the national events, which took place virtually during the month of June. To compete, he had to be videotaped and then have his video posted on YouTube, which allowed SkillsUSA to watch the competition at their leisure. He was graded on safety, individual timed welds for each project, and quality of his work. To complete the competition, a certified welding inspector (CWI) came to Lakeland to verify the welds and their overall appearance.

On June 24, as I interviewed John for this chapter, he told me he was expecting his results from the competition *that day* at 4:00 p.m.! I'm not making this up. We didn't plan the interview to coincide with his results. It just happened.

John texted me later that night—he had placed sixth in the entire nation.

After finishing in the top of the nation, he was asked to try out for the world competition. He competed in the American Welding Society World SkillsUSA Competition and was crowned the number one welder in the nation. He was scheduled to compete in China, but when COVID-19 hit, the competition was shut down. Even though he was not able to compete on the world stage, John has opened many doors to careers in the field of welding.

All of this would not have been possible without a commitment and relentless pursuit to be great. That's exactly how we win in life, by being disciplined daily and focused on becoming the greatest that we can be in the field we are pursuing. All of us must act like John did. Most of us know how to be excellent in our craft, but are we willing to make sacrifices for our desired *great* outcome? Will we build the daily habits of hard work to make our dreams a reality?

Not everyone is going to be as persistent as John. But like the old saying goes, "You reap what you sow."

 **If our daily routines and behaviors consistently demonstrate a dedication to hard work and striving for excellence, our chances of achieving success greatly increase.**

What might you need to change in your life to be great?

RYAN'S RULES:

1. Wake up early, give 100 percent effort to the task, communicate effectively with people, and you'll have great results.

2. Show the world how great you are by daily *doing* the work—not just *talking* about it.

3. Work hard to love one another, to be the best you can be at your craft, and to be a good citizen in your community.

Applied knowledge + Changed behavior = Transformation

CHAPTER 10

—

"I Suck at School"

"I suck at school!" Ryan said to his parents one evening when he was in grade school. "It just doesn't make sense to me, and I can't keep up with the rest of the kids."

COMPARISON IS THE THIEF OF JOY

School is where Ryan started to feel uncomfortable about a lot of things in his life. It wasn't about what he couldn't do; it was about what everybody else thought—that he was stupid.

In kindergarten, first grade, and the beginning of second grade, everything was learned with his hands. Math was learned with apples in hand; one apple in your hand plus two more makes three apples. Kids colored by numbers and used pencils to draw out letters and numbers. He was doing things with his hands.

Then in third grade, children were taught how to put sentences together, how to read them, and how to organize them in paragraphs. By fourth grade, assignments were "Read the chapter and answer questions at the back of the book," and learning—or trying to learn—became an experience that Ryan truly hated as he struggled with his severe dyslexia.

He remembers sitting on the couch with his dad, trying to read paragraph after paragraph, and crying because he couldn't comprehend anything. So he learned to create a mask and started to act goofy in class because it would at least allow people to see him as a person instead of someone who was 'stupid.' During class, he never tried to answer the first questions the teacher asked; his tactic was to learn from the answers other individuals gave. Ryan listened, gathered information from other students' answers, and then prepared what he was going to say if called upon. This method allowed him to be confident if he had to give an answer in front of the class. He knew he wasn't going to get the grades that others were striving for; he only wanted to 'fit in' and get through school without being laughed at.

Through the rest of his years of elementary and high school education, Ryan made use of abilities other than reading and writing. But thinking about what would come after graduation and what life would be like then 'scared the hell' out of him.

He says, "I'm going through high school, and I just didn't think I could amount to anything. I mean, it was like everybody had a vision for me as to what I'm going to do—which was work in a factory or have a basic 'job.' You could create a living with that, but I wanted more. My lack of doing well in school scared me away from wanting to go to college or get a higher education or even join the military because of the ASVAB [an aptitude test used by the military]."

Ryan had not had any wins in education, and the fear of what was next after graduating haunted him. He did know that if he kept working hard and kept on plugging away by just passing his classes, he could at least graduate with a high school diploma and figure out his life when it came to that point.

ADAPTING TO LEARN

Ryan's severe dyslexia is still a factor in his life. Reading for comprehension does not come easily; it's like trying to swim wearing a 50-pound vest! For many of us, schooling may have been easy, or at least not that challenging. For Ryan and the students with disabilities he teaches, it's a suffer-fest for them just to get through each day.

Ryan will never forget the day Mrs. L., a teacher, brought him cassette tapes. "Here, these are for you," she said.

He said, "What are these? I don't listen to music."

She explained that the tapes weren't music but were recordings of her reading the first chapters of his science, history, and health books. He did not have to struggle to read the chapters himself; now he could put the tapes into a recorder and listen to her reading to him.

Wow! Audiobooks didn't exist back then, but what an impact those cassette recordings had on Ryan. Mrs. L., and teachers like her, influenced Ryan's teaching today. He says, "If we do more for these kids who are struggling, make things that aren't easy for them easier, when they become successful, they're going to empower you even more because their success will prove the point that they can do things that everybody else thinks they can't do."

During all his years in school, Ryan never read an entire book. His methods for success were listening to others, trying to read at least the important information in his textbook (with help), and getting as much support as he could at home, from his girlfriend during high school, and from the special education staff at school.

When he went to college to receive his teaching certification, these same methods were still in play. His high-school sweetheart was now his wife, and he'd ask her for help. **He needed others to help him, and if not for their support, he claims, he never would have made it to be where he is today.** He was teaching welding at the same time he was taking college courses, and he tells the story about turning in a homework assignment that looked like it had been done by someone else. It was written in his wife's handwriting.

My professor asked me if I was going to change the handwriting before I turned it in.

I said, "Nope, that's what you're going to get!"

The professor said, "Ryan ... I mean ... you're not even going to change it so it's your own handwriting?"

I replied, "My wife wrote it out for me. I promise; I'm not cheating. It's my thoughts, not hers. But it was just so much easier for me not to go through the pain and suffering of writing it out. I can't write well, and you couldn't read my handwriting."

The professor said, "You know what? I've got to believe you. You're one of the few people in my class who has 100 percent participation in everything we do, and you answer more questions than anybody else in the entire class."

"Another reason is this—" I told her, "I'm so sick and tired of being judged by individuals. I don't know where to use there or their or they're; I can't get the punctuation right, and I don't know how to put everything in the correct order. I didn't want run-on sentences, and I wanted this to sound like my words coming from my mouth onto paper. My wife can do that for me. I can't."

Ryan's confession of his reality and what he had to do to

make it through school, especially college, was pure. He knew and understood what was discussed in class. For his papers and assignments, his wife read articles to him. She wrote his papers as he spoke the ideas. (This was before we had the technology of speech-to-text.)

Ryan avoided failure in his classes by adjusting—and produced results in a nontraditional way. Many other people in that situation may have packed it in because it was too much work to find a process that would allow them to show evidence of their work. Not Ryan. He was determined to get done what needed to be done, to make sure he had the opportunity to teach.

Ryan comes from a military family and exemplifies the United States Marines Corps slogan "Improvise, Adapt, and Overcome!" He now uses his own experience as a student to adjust his methodology in his teaching and his business. He goes beyond teaching only the content or just getting a job done. He's all about creating an environment of love, respect, and hard work. He loves building people up, giving them confidence, sharing experiences with them, and teaching them that the foundation of success is hard work. Because he learned to work around his disability, he has impacted thousands of kids and adults in the past twenty years.

RYAN'S RULES:

1. Adjusting is uncomfortable at times, but it's necessary. You'll grow as a person.

2. Find supportive and loving people to help you accomplish your dreams.

3. Quit comparing yourself to others; comparison is the thief of joy.

4. Improvise, Adapt, and Overcome.

Applied knowledge + Changed behavior = Transformation

CHAPTER 11

The Power of Yes and No

If parents and teachers always say yes to a child, what is the result? A monster is created!

The child is then conditioned to get whatever they want. This can be anything and everything from being allowed to watch whatever shows they want whenever they want to playing video games constantly to being on social media on their phone 24/7. If this behavior is allowed, children never learn what a *no* really means.

The word *no* can have two meanings for children. The first way to interpret "No" is simply "No, you cannot do that." **Being firm with a no for children is healthy because it establishes a boundary line between the adult and the child.** It's not about a power struggle; instead, it is simply stating the fact that something a child wants cannot come to pass. The reasons for an adult saying no to a child can be to keep them from harm (as in crossing a road) or not wanting them to waste an opportunity (as in playing video games instead of playing outside with their friends or family).

A no can be saying a yes to something else. This kind of no is helping young children or even adults to learn a disciplined path to being safe and having structure in their lives. Ask yourself, If I had gotten everything I thought I wanted as a child, would my life right now be better or worse? For example, would you still be here today or be healthy if your parents had not said no to your hanging out with the wrong group of friends?

In this sense, the word no helps to mold a person and keep them on the right track to a fruitful destination.

A great example of saying no to support a yes would be when we try to lose weight. If a person says yes to a training program and diet plan, then they may have to say no to sleeping in or having a bag of their favorite potato chips. So, if you want to say yes to the transformed you, then you have to say no and goodbye to your old habits that are holding you back from the new you.

BEING RELENTLESS TO HEAR A YES

Once a child graduates and moves into the adult world, "No" takes on another meaning and new power. If you hear the word no to something that could benefit you, it doesn't mean that thing is impossible. It means you have to find another way. If people continued to hear the word *no* as a firm denial and believed what the other person was saying, nothing would ever be accomplished. "Just because somebody says it can't be done doesn't mean it can't be done," says Ryan. "Let's figure out how to do it another way. That's when I started to look at this incredible opportunity to teach these young men and women what the power and potential of the word *no* is."

"No" may take many different forms. When you're relying on a friend and expecting him to be there or expecting his help, and then something suddenly happens—an emergency or 'life' interferes—that's a form of a no. Does it mean that since they can't help you today, you can't do it? Not at all because life must go on. When we face this kind of no, we have to be able to say, *All right. Let's go down a different path and try to get the same results.*

Ryan gives another example. Sometimes he and his students needed donations for community service projects at school, and a business would tell them no all day long. But when he taught his students how to communicate, collaborate, and educate the community businesses and industries on why they wanted a donation, businesses never told them no. He taught students to call businesses and say, "Hey, we're doing this community service project, and here's the story behind it, and this is who it's going to impact and why it's going to help people and why it's a great opportunity not only for our community but also for our nation." Students learned to conduct intelligent conversations with adult figures, and their approach also caused those businesses to look at these kids and say, *Wow. That's exactly the kid I need to help out and benefit our community.*

This has happened numerous times when Ryan teaches service-learning projects and allows his students to fight past the word *no* and to persevere by communicating clearly with business owners or managers. **The door may initially be shut, but resilience and continued communication is the way to turn a no into a yes.** This skill is very important for everyone who believes in their mission and wants to have success.

NEGATIVE IMPACTS OF SAYING YES

If we never say no to opportunities and people, our constant yes can have a negative impact. Many adults say yes to so many people—to too many people! Then they start to feel overwhelmed because they have added more items to their plate, and anxiety and stress begin to build up. Major mental and physical health concerns can appear. Trying to please people by saying yes can have the opposite effect, and the outcome can be catastrophic.

Therefore, find the delicate balance of knowing how much you can take on your plate. The best method I have found in my journey of life is that every time I say yes to something, I need to stop (say no to) a previous activity.

For example, I recently became the athletic director at my children's school, and I had to make the decision to step down as the head varsity golf coach. Could I have made them both work? Possibly, but when we spread ourselves too thin, we cannot be as effective in every area. **Sacrifices must be made so that we can do an excellent job in one area instead of an average job in two.**

To conclude, a *no* in some contexts is for our safety and to keep us on a healthy path. A *no* that blocks us from doing something means we need to find another way to get the results we want. It's important to say yes to opportunities in life; it can lead to growth and many more great opportunities. But in order to avoid overburdening ourselves and to live a balanced and fulfilling life, we need to responsibly manage how many tasks or roles we take on.

RYAN'S RULES:

1. Be firm with *no* for children. Establish that boundary.

2. Recognize that a *no* doesn't mean something can't be done. Find another way to get the results you want.

3. Learn to communicate effectively after an initial no.

4. Say no when your plate is already full.

Applied knowledge + Changed behavior = Transformation

CHAPTER 12

—

Security Blankets

We have traveled with Ryan through his story, and we know that he struggled with learning. During those difficult years of school, he was called 'dummy' and 'stupid.' **He could have listened to the haters and believed what the world told him about who he was. Instead, he surrounded himself with people who cared about and loved him.**

Ryan calls these people his 'security blankets' in life. He says, "Security blankets are people who know me and know when I don't know how to operate in a specific area in my life. There are potholes and bad weather that can deter my path in life. There are lots of sugars in the gas tank that can spoil the way my engine runs. I am the engine, but my security blankets have allowed me to run to my full potential."

RYAN'S SECURITY BLANKETS

Ryan's wife, Heather, is the person closest to him. She

planted seeds of hope within him and believed that he was going to do amazing things in life because of his work ethic and heart of gold. She saw more in him than he ever saw in himself. With this showering of love and support from her, his roots began to grow stronger and deeper in the soil of that belief, and he began to prosper. His success didn't happen overnight, but the main reason it even began was due to the love and support that he received each day from Heather.

Ryan's parents have always been very strong supporters of him. They molded him into a fine man and taught him the foundational behaviors of believing in oneself, never giving up, and always working hard. His parents raised a son who went through many trials and tribulations, specifically in school, but they were always there to give him a hug or a positive word to encourage him to keep going.

One of Ryan's first students in high school was Phil Henry. Phil is a co-owner with Ryan at their fabrication business. As a former student, Phil showed Ryan that if you work hard and use your talents, you can become successful in your craft. He helps Ryan daily with managing and working on projects for Ryan's company.

During the middle of Ryan's tenure as a teacher, two specific people who helped his journey were Sue and Tom Roseum. Sue taught chemistry and physics at Auburn Career Center, obtained her National Board Certification, and later taught at South High School in Willoughby-East-lake before becoming the Director of the Career Academy (Tech Center). Sue was the administrator Ryan had always wanted to have. She mentored and supported Ryan during his teaching career and demonstrated that if you trust your employees with what they are doing for kids, the sky is the limit in a classroom.

Tom, Sue's husband, was a Career and Technology educator in the field of carpentry. He also had a profound impact on Ryan and helped him navigate problems in teaching and learning how to effectively communicate with everyone. Ryan leaned on Tom for true guidance, and Tom has always provided wisdom in decision-making processes.

Rich Basinski was Ryan's administrator at his local community college. He has been an important supporter and security blanket for Ryan ever since Ryan stepped into the community college. One beautiful story about Rich is about the day he called Ryan into his office and told him to stop sending emails to people he communicated with as an educator.

Ryan replied, "That would be great, but how am I going to communicate with people?"

Rich said, "I will send the emails for you. I am sick and tired of people thinking you are not a smart guy because you can't use the correct their or capitalize your words correctly and punctuate where it's necessary. I know it is difficult for you to write, so I am going to help you with your emails."

Ryan was shocked. Rich was one of the very few administrators who understood his disability and wanted to take positive action so Ryan wouldn't have to worry about how people would interpret his emails—and make judgments about him.

Ryan says,

> *My number one blanket is John Grdina because he is the fender, the cab, the hood, the trunk, and the bed of my truck that makes it looks pretty and allows me to store stuff in the back that are ideas for future opportunities. He is the guy who puts it all together to make all the parts of the vehicle run smoothly. He has been with me for eighteen years and knows how I function; he's been there and seen it all. He has done a microscope dive into my heart and has supported me because he knew I wasn't crazy but had a heart to love people and show them how much I care for them.*

I truly am a blessed man to help Ryan maneuver through many unique challenges and circumstances in his life. I have always seen something special in him, and maybe it's as simple as him having a heart of gold for others. He has never done activities—especially as a teacher—in the conventional way, but that's what makes his special engine sauce run each day. He's always there to push people to be the best and to achieve the highest that they can, whether that is in welding, another career field, or simply being a human being. I'm honored to be his security blanket.

BE A SECURITY BLANKET

Ryan is an excellent communicator. Not only can he explain ideas, concepts, and the 'why' behind something, but he also understands how to bring value to others around him. Talking with him, a person feels supported and cared for. He has become a security blanket for others.

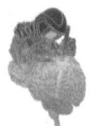 **Parents, nowhere is it more important to provide love, support, and security than at home.**

Ryan has poured out love and support for his family. He not only preaches and practices this blueprint daily in his career, but he also demonstrates this with his children (Austin, Samantha, and Sarah) as well. As a result, Ryan's son, Austin, is now the general manager of all the employees at Ryan's business, Arc-Hound Welding and Fabrication. From Ryan, Austin has learned the importance of having a work ethic and doing things for the community. He has learned how to be an effective leader and has earned this responsibility in the business.

During high school, Austin attained Eagle Scout rank, which is a high honor and a rare feat these days because it is a challenge that requires earning 21 merit badges. These are the actions a Boy Scout must take in order to earn the high rank of Eagle Scout:

> *Earn a total of 21 merit badges (10 more than required for the Life rank), including these 13 merit badges: (a) First Aid, (b) Citizenship in the Community, (c) Citizenship in the Nation, (d) Citizenship in the World, (e) Communication, (f) Cooking, (g) Personal Fitness, (h) Emergency Preparedness OR Lifesaving, (i) Environmental Science OR Sustainability, (j) Personal Management, (k) Swimming OR Hiking OR Cycling, (l) Camping, and (m) Family Life.*

As a young man, he recalls, "My dad pushed me hard to do good and not mess up. He wanted the best for me, and he expected a lot out of me. I didn't realize then how to be successful—but I do now. When I was in my late teens, I didn't know if I could live up to the excellence of some of his (Ryan's) students, but I've stopped looking at them as competition and instead see them as part of the family that my dad created through his teaching."

During his teenage years, Austin had difficulty deciding what to do with his life. But after thinking about his future and his legacy, he couldn't see any other way of living his life except to be alongside his dad on this journey. His integrity and humility allow him to learn from his dad and older individuals without feeling resentment toward them.

After high school, Austin hit the road, literally. For almost five years, he traveled all over the country as a union boilermaker, grinding out long days and independently learning what it took to be a very productive welder. When Ryan planned to start a fabrication business, he wanted Austin to play a pivotal role in the company. Austin made the career move because he knew Ryan puts his whole heart into everything he does, and Austin wanted to work with his dad to be a part of creating a new welding empire. He also knew that past students of his father would be working at this company, and he knew this was an opportunity he couldn't pass up.

All of us need to surround ourselves with excellent individuals who will help us grow and hold us accountable to be the next best version of ourselves. My hope is that you have at least one security blanket in your life helping you navigate the terrain of this beautiful journey.

RYAN'S RULES:

1. Make the effort daily to build people up and make them feel loved and valued.

2. Be a beacon of hope and light to others.

3. To experience a sense of fulfillment, engage in selfless acts of kindness without any expectations or reciprocity.

Applied knowledge + Changed behavior = Transformation

CHAPTER 13

———

"When Am I Ever Going to Use This?"

Have you ever sat in class and said to yourself, "When am I ever going to use this?"

I know Ryan and I have. So why it is that so many of us go through school and don't understand why we are learning specific content?

Students most often ask this when they see a lack of immediate relevance. They may find it difficult to connect what they are learning in class to their current experiences and their future goals. **If they can't see how the knowledge or skills will be useful to them, then why should they learn it?**

Another factor is limited perspective. Students have limited knowledge about the vast range of careers or fields currently in the world. They may not understand how certain subjects can be applied in various professions.

Students may also question what they are learning because explanations have been unclear. Sometimes teachers are not effective in communicating the relevance of a topic; this can lead to confusion and the perception that the subject is unnecessary.

"When am I ever going to use this?" may also come out of a fear of failure. Some students, especially those who may be suffering at school, might ask this question almost daily as a defense mechanism to avoid the challenges or potential failures associated with learning difficult or complex subjects.

With all these reasons why students ask the question, how can educators, parents, and community stakeholders help students gain relevancy in what they are learning?

Again, we can learn from Ryan's experience and journey. He explains how many kids will go through their educational experience struggling and therefore think they are bad students. That's not true. They must understand how to adapt and learn differently. Many kids learn not by "reading the chapter and answering the questions at the back of the book" but by using their hands. Those kids need to learn how awesome it is to build something with your hands—and get credit for it.

Sadly, when industrial arts and home economics classes were taken out of educational platforms, we took away opportunities from those individuals who don't learn by reading chapters and writing answers to questions. Those students could never feel their potential or that they were gaining strengths. That's why some kids who have a learning disability are very good at sports. That's where they thrive. And for many of them who have to get passing grades to play sports, it's hard just to get the grade to be qualified to play the game that they love.

When students who learn differently can get into a career/technical educational program, parents will come to the teachers in gratitude and say, "Where have you been? My kid's never gotten an A in anything. And now he's thriving!" Because now math is relevant. Now reading an instruction manual is relevant. Students understand that if they learn this material and can use their hands to build stuff to get a grade, learning is exciting and relevant. We have seen kids who were straight D students become straight A students in their eleventh-grade year. And everybody's like, *How was this possible?*

To foster a sense of curiosity and relevancy in learning, **educators need to provide real-world examples by illustrating the connections between subjects and practical applications.**

Making education fun and relevant and attaching a vision to the student's future occupation are great strategies to ensure an exciting outlook on their futures. If teachers continue to teach, and possibly just 'teach to the test,' day in and day out, would you be excited to go to school each day?

Probably not, but if there was someone who talked to you after the lecture and taught in a manner that made learning engaging, how much more would you not only want to be at school but also engage in the content?

In a Greek mythology class, Ryan had a teacher who made learning fun for everyone. Every year, Mrs. K. would have the class pick a Greek mythology character and create a costume for that god or goddess. Then, when she was teaching about that specific character, she would wear the costume that a previous year's class had made for that character. Creating and making the costumes added fun and relevance to learning the content of the class.

As educators, we must make the relevance of math and English clear so our students understand exactly what skills these subjects will give them and how they'll be using those skills in everyday life and society. When Ryan talks about fabricating something, for example, he also talks about geometry and figuring out angles, and when he's building projects, he teaches SOH-CAH-TOA and specific formulas in math, showing students the applications and why this knowledge is beneficial to making the project a success. "I literally show them that here is an angle or here's a joist that goes into a house, and here's how we figure out these angles. If I'm going to be in the construction field, I need to know how to use math to be able to measure, and I need to know how to figure out radiuses and circumferences and diameters."

It's important for educators to be able to create something to show the why of learning Math and English and Science. That's relevance. Teachers, it's so important to be able to use your life stories so students can understand how learning is going to relate to life and how they're going to be able to use it in the future. If you can show them why a subject is important for a project's success, they will be 100 percent more engaged.

LEARNING THROUGH FAILURE

Another concept that I have learned in education is that **we must teach the students how to make mistakes.** Many parents are looking at their child's grades, and if they don't get an A in a course, they feel defeated. I must tell you, a D and a C are often ten times better than an A. Many people don't understand that.

So many kids have not 'learned' how to make a mistake. **Making a mistake is how growth occurs.** Making a mistake is how common sense is gained. If you didn't get the right answer, the right grade, the right appearance, or the right result, you now have found out what doesn't work. So, you've got to find a different way. If a student is disappointed because she got a D, she has learned how not to do something. But if she wants to get better in a subject, she will have to learn how to do something differently. She'll know that if she never wants to see a D again, she'll have to learn to correct the mistakes she made in the first place.

But what does our society today teach kids to do? Wait for somebody else to come and give them the answer! Young people so often are not given an opportunity to think and dig deeper and figure out something on their own. When there is a problem, many people don't know how to find a solution because they are afraid to try something and be wrong. So, while we give some guidance along the way, we must allow students or people who are learning their craft to work through trial and error.

People learn in different ways, but being passionate about what you are teaching and engaging students with what they are learning is vital for increased engagement and outlook for their future. Learning can be exciting when students know where they are headed, but **with no vision, passion, and application of knowledge, well then, they are just going through the system of education zombie-like, moving down an assembly line.**

One of my favorite quotes is from William Arthur Ward, an inspirational writer:

 **"The mediocre teacher tells. The good teacher explains. The superior teacher demonstrates. The great teacher inspires."**

RYAN'S RULES:

1. Don't be afraid of making mistakes. Mistakes can lead to growth.

2. Educators provide real-world examples illustrating the connection between subjects and practical applications.

3. Don't judge people for what they do not know; instead, help people who want to get better and stick with them on their journey toward success.

Applied knowledge + Changed behavior = Transformation

CHAPTER 14

—

Be You!

'Just being you' means that you are going to do so many things in life that other people won't agree with. You'll meet people who have different views and who believe that you 'should' live a certain way, according to their perspective.

Ryan has been told not to do this or that because someone felt it would hurt his career. He would look at the person telling him "You can't" and say, "Well, let me try, and we will see what happens." **If no one gets hurt or goes to jail, why not try something you feel passionate about?**

As you have learned, Ryan has lived his life in a non-conventional manner. To be himself in school, he had to use his athletic ability to show the other kids that he was worthy of being someone. Fast forwarding to years after school, Ryan didn't change who he was, a fun-loving, big-hearted guy who loves people. He just had to find a place where he could unlock his treasures of talents.

A superpower was awakened when he learned not only how to weld but to how to teach people to weld. This was the point in his life when he found his calling and became the truest version of himself. In teaching welding, he could just be Ryan in the fullest sense because he combined his talents (speaking and developing people) with his new skill (welding). Ryan was born into his element and life's calling when these two areas met.

Today, when Ryan is in his welding school, he is constantly analyzing students' strengths for specific fields (Construction, Manufacturing, Fabrication, and Inspection). With the understanding that not every person coming into his school is created to be a welder, he helps these young men and women by identifying their strengths and passions and then connects them with local industries that would be a great match for both parties and where they can contribute in a pivotal role. For example, an individual who is not the best welder or fabricator but who can communicate effectively and ask the right questions can find a path to be a leader for a company or small business. **Ryan has a gift of recognizing people's unique talents and has always helped direct them into a pathway of prosperity.**

DON'T BE A BOB

Think about your life. Are you using your talents and skills to do something you have a passion for? Or are you 'just working a job' because it pays the bills? It's a shame that many of us go into a career based solely on the wages and benefits provided rather than pursuing a career that makes use of our talents and is based on our true passion.

Let's look at an example; we'll call him 'Bob.' He worked at a job where he was paid $100,000 each year and had great benefits (health care, 401k, sick leave, etc.). The only problem was that Bob hated to go to work each day because it did not support his mission in life. Bob's passion was creating art and discussing with people the beauties of all the art in the world. Instead, he was working at a job on an assembly line, putting together parts.

Let's imagine that Bob learned how to use his talents and skills and create his own company. He had the background to create and innovate various products, and he has always loved talking to people. So how come Bob couldn't get outside his comfort zone and *do it*?

It was money and security that kept Bob working on the assembly line, making good money—and not fulfilling his life's purpose. He retired in his late sixties and had poor health shortly after. Unfortunately, he passed away just five years after retirement and took all his ideas, talents, and passions to the grave.

You don't have to be like Bob. Instead, you can start working on yourself now to determine what type of job you want with the talents you already have. When you use those talents alongside a skill you are passionate about, then boom! You are in your calling.

 **Do not worry about the money factor. Being fulfilled and being you in your journey of life will make it a sweet journey.**

BE AUTHENTIC TO YOU

Educators, parents, and mentors, it is our job to find the strengths of our young people to mold them into careers that fit individual gifts and personalities. We need to look at kids as chocolate and melt them down to fit their own specific mold instead of trying to pour them all into one mold and *make* them fit. Kids in Ryan's classes are put into a career position that takes shape from his observations about each individual as they go through his welding class. He helps them to not only be a welder but to also be a worker who fits the right career based on their talents, strengths, and passions.

We must understand that education does not have to look like an assembly line. Instead, it can be a beautiful maturation process where the student starts to understand their unique talents and passions and where observation by a teacher, parent, or mentor gives guidance as to what profession may be the best fit. What should not happen is that a specific career field is chosen only because it is the family tradition or because someone else wants the young person to follow a certain path.

Important concepts for young and old alike—for students and teachers, parents, or mentors—are being authentic, accepting ourselves, finding fulfillment, building authentic connections, pursuing personal growth, and being inspired and inspiring.

Authenticity is being true to ourselves. This in turn allows us to live a life that aligns with our values, beliefs, and personal identity. It allows us to express our genuine thoughts, feelings, and desires, leading to a sense of inner peace and congruence.

Self-acceptance is embracing who we are. That includes our strengths, weaknesses, quirks, and imperfections. Self-acceptance allows us to develop a positive self-image and cultivate self-compassion, both of which are crucial for mental and emotional well-being.

Personal growth and self-development can only come when we embrace our authentic selves. The desire for growth encourages us to explore our passions, talents, and interests, pushing us to continually learn, evolve, and expand our horizons.

Fulfillment is a result of being true to ourselves and pursuing activities, relationships, and goals that genuinely resonate with us. This leads to greater satisfaction in life, as we are actively engaged in meaningful pursuits.

Authentic connections are relationships in which we can be ourselves with people who appreciate and accept us for who we are. We form genuine connections and build relationships based on mutual understanding, trust, and respect.

Inspiration is a gift that is naturally passed on. We may be the inspiration others need. Watching us live authentically and confidently can encourage them to embrace their own uniqueness and pursue their dreams without fear of judgment or societal expectations.

Being yourself is a continuous journey of self-discovery and self-acceptance. Living a life that is true to who you are leads to greater happiness, fulfillment, and transformational growth.

RYAN'S RULES:

1. Don't be a Bob.

2. Make choices that align with your values, beliefs, and personal identity.

3. Find the place and path where you can unlock your treasures of talents.

4. Nurture relationships in which you can be you.

Applied knowledge + Changed behavior = Transformation

CHAPTER 15

You Don't Know What You Don't Know

Growing up, I lived in a Midwest suburb outside of Cleveland, Ohio, and everyone was pretty much like me and my family. I knew little about diversity—other foods, cultures, and how other people lived. It wasn't until I went to college that I understood that there are many other belief systems out there, as well as diversity of cultures. I lived in a bubble my entire childhood.

Awareness is a powerful tool. The more aware you become, the more you'll find thousands of jobs out there that you have never heard about or have not researched. The more aware you become of differences in people, culture, and beliefs, the more likely you will be able to understand where people are coming from and not feel nervous or afraid to communicate with people who may not look like you or act like you. The more aware you become, even of your own belief system, the more likely you are to make better decisions for yourself.

 **Thus, awareness is the first step to unlocking doors of wisdom.**

Ryan and I had a candid conversation about becoming more aware of yourself and what's out there. We reflected on our role as educators and mentors in helping young people gain awareness. Our job is to teach them in the present day about their future and show them who they can become. Kids come into Ryan's program, and he gets to see something special—for the first time, they thrive. Outside the confines of a school desk, they become aware that learning can be fun, and their teacher guides them in gaining experience and knowledge of all the possibilities that the trades offer.

We also have the opportunity to further the awareness of parents. In parent-teacher conferences, we get to meet the parents of the young men and women we're teaching. These parents or guardians have been a part of the child's life but may not even know their child's strengths. Ryan delights in the opportunity he's given: "So I have a chance to tell them their son or daughter is doing amazing things and has developed new strengths and experiences. Then I make their parents aware of all the wonderful knowledge the kid has acquired in welding and fabrication and what specific field I feel would be best for them based on their specific talents and strengths."

What we have learned as educators is that, ultimately, **'molding' an individual's mind is shaping them so they become aware of their strengths and their ability to achieve in the trades, industries, or any specific career that they are seeking.**

THE RIPPLE EFFECT OF MOLDING MINDS

As educators and mentors, we also have the opportunity to share with students our own experiences so they don't have to make the same mistakes we did. Learning from people who have gone through the gauntlet of life experiences will help forge character. With our experiences and all the people we've met and the things we've been doing in our lives to better ourselves, our family, and our community, we're here to teach young people, "Guess what? It's possible. You can do it too."

Young people, we need you to do this for two reasons: **You need to become the best version of yourself by unleashing all your potential. Secondly, when you understand your talent and what you are passionate about and work on it daily, you feel fulfilled.** I wish I had known this secret earlier in life so that my brain would have been molded (awakened) to this knowledge long before it actually was.

The best part is, if you are reading this, you have heard the truth of how to live a fulfilled life. Use your talents and combine them with something you are passionate about, and then, *Bam*! The life you dreamed of will become a reality, and you will live with purpose. Unfortunately, many people have not learned this simple formula or their belief system has been skewed by environmental factors, and thus, they do not live by these concepts. Just remember, don't waste what you now know for the rest of your life!

Ryan tells a funny story about not knowing what you don't know, and he tells it so well that I'll give it to you in his own words:

I'm driving some young men to a competition. We're driving down a highway, and there's a field, and out in the middle of this field, there's a cow. One young man says, "What's that?"

"What do you mean … *what's that?*" I ask. "That's a cow."

He says, "Oh, wow. I've never seen a cow before."

And I say, "You've never seen a cow before?" That's the craziest thing I ever heard in my life. This is a twelfth-grader in high school!

So what do I do? I find the next exit, pull off, and drive for 45 minutes to find a cow. We finally find another cow in the middle of an Amish field, and we take pictures of it. And it is the craziest thing because I think he's joking. Never seen a cow before? "Not a live cow," he says. He's seen them on TV.

And I'm like, "You're nuts."

So we got back in the car and go to the competition and have this great day. We're driving back, and the cow is still on my mind.

I'm like, "Man, I can't believe you've never seen a cow before."

And he looks at me, and he says, "Hey E, can I ask you a question?"

"Sure. What's up?"

He says, "I might not have ever seen a cow, but let me ask you this. Have you ever seen a dead body, or have you ever been in a drive-by shooting?"

"No, sir," I say.

"I have," he says.

Let's put stuff in perspective. So, so many of these young men and women are growing up in such a different environment than I. I am so sheltered as to how some people live, and they are so unaware of the way I live. It's just unbelievable. We just don't know what others have experienced without having walked a mile in their shoes. And if we can't break down those barriers and break down those walls, we do a disservice to our students and fellow man if, at first, we judge.

So, as people who want to become better individuals and be people of character, we need to have more humility, work hard, judge less, love more, and do things passionately.

RYAN'S RULES:

1. Embrace opportunities to experience diverse cultures.

2. At the very least, be open to conversations with people who are not like you, who live differently and have different belief systems.

3. Learn from people who have gone through the gauntlet of life experiences.

4. Ask a trusted teacher, parent, or mentor what potential and strengths they see in you waiting to be unleashed.

Applied knowledge + Changed behavior = Transformation

CHAPTER 16

Unanswered Prayers

I wanted to marry my high school sweetheart, and I went to college to invest in our relationship and future. During that entire time of five-plus years, I prayed that the stars would align and that we would one day be at the altar together and start a family soon thereafter.

Well, God did not answer my prayer to be with this young lady. Instead, shortly after a very difficult breakup, He brought a new woman into my life, and she would eventually become my wife.

Have you ever sat up late at night praying for your dream to come true? Or have you been in a desperate situation and prayed there would be a way out?

I am sure that all of us have been in some situation like this. Some of you may currently be in the same situation I was in, praying for a relationship to work out the way you want it to, but you also know it is not heading in the direction that you are praying for. Garth Brooks wrote about this in an epic country hit, "Unanswered Prayers," and described so well what we have all experienced. If you have a chance, listen to it now.

You may be in circumstances right now that you feel will never work out. It may be problems with an alcoholic parent or an abusive family member or a difficult relationship you are in. You may have prayed about your current situation and even got mad at God for not making life the way you would like it to be.

Ryan and I would tell you that we have experienced some of the most depressing and disappointing moments—from failing tests to not getting into the military to not marrying the girl of our dreams. In these trials, we both possessed one distinct character trait: Faith.

When Ryan's high school dreams of joining the military were dashed by his fall and injuries while rock climbing in the Garden of the Gods, he held to his faith that something would work itself out for him. **He believed that if he worked hard and was 'just himself,' he would find a profession that would be a perfect fit.** Indeed, that is exactly what happened. He put his nose to the grindstone, worked at Lincoln Electric, took classes to learn how to weld, and then the magic happened! The instructors become aware of his amazing ability, not only in welding but also in interacting with others.

When jobs, relationships, or deals don't go their way, most

people just stop and 'simply settle.' How many times in your life have you not got what you dreamed of and then just settled? Or said, "Well, I guess this wasn't the way it was supposed to be ..."?

People 'settle' because they don't have faith and a strong enough belief that good things will be attracted to them if they just continue to do the work. Instead of settling, **we need to act on being the best versions of ourselves by getting out of our head of regret, fear, and misery, and embracing moving forward with resilience, work ethic, and gratitude for where we are headed.** If we would just move forward with actions that reflect our passions, we would start gaining traction in the right direction.

Ryan and I are no better than anyone else reading this book. We are very successful in our careers, and we each have a loving family surrounding us.

 **We won't settle because we work hard, believe good things are always around the corner, and build strong relationships with people.**

THE COMPOUND EFFECT

If you want to start living your best life, take a first step by simply doing what you say you are going to do, and you will begin to unlock doors to new opportunities. For example, if you want to be the best salesperson, make two more calls per day. If you did this repeatedly, you would make 10 more calls per week, 40 more calls per month, and 520 more calls per year! The compound effect of just two more calls daily would mean 520 more calls per year, putting you in the driver's seat to more sales.

Or you could be a person who thinks your life is not going in the direction you want, and so you will do less in almost every area of your life, thus making strides in the wrong direction. For example, let's say you eat when you're depressed, and now you eat 500 more calories per day. 500 calories are just a plain bagel with cream cheese. You have an extra bagel each day, compounding to 3,500 extra calories per week and a whopping 182,000 calories per year! You're not living a healthy lifestyle, and as a result, you are most likely gaining weight in the process.

Little habits, good or bad, can change the momentum of wherever you are heading. So, simply put, **start tracking some small habits that will benefit you daily and take you toward the destination you want and stop habits that are holding you back from being the transformed you!**

It's your choice. Daily!

HAVE FAITH

You may be praying for something big to happen in your life—a new job, a restored relationship, or the house of your dreams. You should be praying that all these desires come to fruition, but you must know that it may not turn out the way you intended. Instead, if you have faith, continue to work hard on your dreams, and never give up, the outcome will be even better!

Once you let doubt creep in because God didn't answer your prayers, well then, my friend, you won't move toward the transformed you; instead, you will slip further backward, toward a version of you that you never wanted.

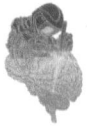 **To make your path in life prosperous, know that not every prayer has to be answered your way, but instead, have faith that God will provide even more than you could ever have imagined!**

RYAN'S RULES:

1. What habits are holding you back from moving toward the new you? Say no to them daily.

2. Start tracking some small habits that will take you to where you want to go.

3. Do what you say you are going to do!

Applied knowledge + Changed behavior = Transformation

CHAPTER 17

Learn the Game

Ryan is a department coordinator at Lakeland Community College, and he says it's amazing that they allow him to do what he has been doing there for the last fourteen years— without a degree. They believe in him. They allow him to keep teaching individuals to become the best well-rounded citizens in our society. He says, "It is my job as an educator to not lie to anyone who comes to my program. I don't tell them that they can go out and do whatever they want. My job is to identify what their strengths are and teach them how to love their strengths so they can become the best individuals that they possibly can be."

Once students finish the welding program, he helps to align them with a job in a fabrication facility, at a construction site, or with a motorsports business. Some students may never weld but will be the best material handler, the best fitter, the best technician, the best press brake operator, or the best laser programmer. **It's our job as educators to identify where they're going to fit into society so they can succeed.**

From that entry point on a new job, his students have learned to "work their butts off and make a name for themselves." Eventually, a business owner or manager might ask on a job, "Hey, anybody know how to do this type of welding?" And a student Ryan taught would say, "I learned it back in school. I think I can ..."

If you can make yourself resourceful, then you've learned the game of life. The more that you can offer to a business, family, or community, the greater edge you have over everyone else. You not only provide the skills for your specific trade, but you are also a 'universal' worker who provides much value to others by having knowledge of multiple disciplines.

RELATIONSHIPS AND RESOURCES

Ryan will often get a phone call or text from a former student asking a question about how to weld or fabricate something for their work. Ryan responds with answers or advice and sometimes even has the former student come to his high school or shop so he can *show* them how to do it. A humble leader with a heart of gold, Ryan has established strong relationships with the students, relationships in which they know that they can trust Ryan to help them.

 **Building a relationship with your teacher, professor, or mentor can lead to a lifetime of knowledge and wisdom.**

Reach out to seek the wisdom of others.

How many times do we go through life thinking we can do it all on our own? Or say to ourselves, *I will figure it out?* Yes, there are times to try to learn on your own and learn from your mistakes, but how much time would you save if you reached out to a friend, family member, or former teacher who has more knowledge and experience than you?

This is why it is so important to establish strong relationships with people in your life.

FRONT BRAKES

I planned on fixing the front brakes on my van. This was something that I had not done in over a decade, but my pride took over, and I was on a mission to accomplish this job in just a few hours.

After being stuck with bolts seized, I had to reach out to a friend who I knew had experience working on cars. I called him up and said, "I can't get these bolts off for the life of me and have been trying for the past hour."

He replied, "I'll be right over, John."

Gerard came over and had two essential resources that I didn't—a breaker bar and spray to soak the bolts. He said, "Spray the bolts, wait an hour, then use the breaker bar, and you should be all set."

"That's it?" I replied.

"Yep."

A simple phone call to ask Gerard for help saved me hours of frustration and physical strain, in addition to avoiding family frustration at my wasting hours on a job that I had pridefully said I could do in a short time.

Build up your skills and relationships so that you can learn the game of life, which is to use resources (people, products, knowledge) in varied and unique situations. The more we can capitalize on relationships and resources, the better we can move forward with projects and, more importantly, be a resource for someone else.

RYAN'S RULES:

1. Identify the specific area where you will fit into society and succeed.

2. Build long-lasting relationships.

3. Reach out to seek the wisdom of others.

Applied knowledge + Changed behavior = Transformation

CHAPTER 18

Failure is the Way

The 'crazy' thing (in Ryan's words) about him is that he's been awarded an honor as a college educator of the year—and he does not have a college degree.

Every time he tried to get some type of credential to say that he was 'worthy' of teaching and doing what he does, he fell short. He wanted to qualify for his CWI (certified welding inspector), but he did not pass the exam. He was half a percent off! He needed 72 percent to pass, and he got 71. One question missed kept him from certification. He was shocked, rocked, and couldn't believe it. One question missed, and he did not have the credential to 'prove' that he had the welding knowledge and 'deserved' respect.

SUCCESS IS MORE THAN A TITLE OR CERTIFICATION

Ryan has done amazing things with kids and adults, training them to be well-rounded citizens and top welders. He and his students have won national championships.

He's also an education consultant who has won numerous awards, including AWS National Educator of the Year. With all of these accolades and teaching other instructors all over the world, Ryan has done it all without a piece of paper or letters behind his name that say "higher education." He does what he does to show other people that it is possible to be successful without degrees, titles, or certifications.

The only title next to his name is 'L.D.' When he does keynote speaking or educational consulting, he introduces himself as Ryan Eubank, L.D.

LITTLE DUMMY TO LEARNING DIFFERENT

L.D., as you have learned, meant 'Little Dummy' as Ryan was growing up, but as the years have passed, he has given those letters a new meaning. Now he understands that they mean 'Learning Differently.' All of us learn best in a certain way, and we have failed countless times as we try to find our 'niche' or our skill. None of us are dumb or stupid; instead, we all learn differently, and for some, it's easier than for others.

Ryan says that those two letters, L.D., are the coolest two letters he could have attached to his name. He realizes how amazing it is that he has accomplished everything he has, and he will always acknowledge and be grateful for the amazing men and women who believed in him and supported him on his path in life as Ryan Eubank, L.D.

RESILIENCY IS FORGED THROUGH FAILURE

Ryan still finds it hard to believe that the trajectory of his journey has brought him to where he is today, proud of what he's accomplished and of what is ahead for his life. And all his failures and setbacks? Those trials, he says, are what made him who he is today.

Failure is part of what makes us who we are. The difference between the person who fails but is still successful and the person who does not succeed is that the successful person learns from their mistakes. After a failure or setback, they adjust to see a new path for how their life could look. Instead of getting upset that they failed in school or failed to finish a race in the time they wanted, they find a new way to accomplish their mission.

I raced in my first ultra-marathon in 2020, the Bigfoot 50K. I thought I was ready since I had completed three other marathons that year—but boy was I wrong.

I ran the race, which consisted of 3 loops of a little more than 10 miles per loop. The course was in the woods for 6 miles, with difficult terrain of mud, hills, and roots. After climbing out of the woods, the last four miles were over flowing hills, and then the race ended with two large inclines on a golf course cart path.

Halfway through the race, I noticed that I didn't have enough supplies to fill my calorie and electrolyte intake, as

I was depleting these while sweating. The last loop was literally a loop through hell physically and mentally. I bonked so bad that I was hallucinating, and I had the worst mindset imaginable because I didn't have the nutrition needed to sustain me during the race.

My mind raced to negative thoughts about quitting and getting a ride back on an ATV, but I decided to gut it out.

I finished the race in seven hours, got in my car, and my dad drove us back home. My body completely seized up with cramps. I was in the worst pain I'd ever experienced. I buried my head in a pillow I had brought and vowed never to do something like this again!

That failure to run a good race in the Bigfoot 50K taught me the greatest lessons of being an ultra-runner. My failure taught me that I need to always bring extra electrolytes and calories because I can't rely on aid stations to have them for me. It also taught me that I need to train more hills before tackling a course with lots of elevation. Lastly, the race taught me that WE are more capable than we can imagine.

These lessons during a race where my body failed taught me that I can run long distances if I have the right plan in place, with mileage ramping, heart-rate training, more training on hills, and the right nutrition. If it wasn't for what I learned from this disastrous race, I would not have completed a 100-mile race and a treadmill race with 28,251 feet of elevation in less than one day.

 **I learned that failure teaches us great lessons, and when we apply the knowledge gained, we can do the unthinkable!**

So, if you have failed in something—good! This means that you can learn and grow from your failure. The more you fail, the more you learn how not to do something. Therefore, continue to fail, and continue to learn. With what you learn, adapt, and then continue your pursuit to live the greatest life imagined!

RYAN'S RULES:

1. Ask yourself if you are allowing a past failure to defeat you in a present opportunity—and if you will continue to *choose* to let it defeat you.

2. Reject the idea that a title behind your name will mean you're an expert.

3. Think about your most recent setback. Ask yourself, "What can I learn from this? How can I adapt and move ahead?"

Applied knowledge + Changed behavior = Transformation

CHAPTER 19

Theoretical vs. Practical

"People are either theoretical or practical learners, and if you're both theoretical and practical, you're considered a genius." —Ryan Eubank

As a Master Shepherd, Ryan not only looks for the strengths each student brings to the table; he also studies what type of learner each person is, either theoretical or practical.

 **A theoretical learner is an individual who excels in understanding and applying abstract concepts and theories.**

They have a strong preference for learning through reading, studying, and analyzing information rather than hands-on or practical experiences. Theoretical learners generally thrive in academic environments where they can explore complex ideas, engage in critical thinking, and dig into principles and theories of a particular subject.

Practical learners are individuals who learn best through hands-on experiences and physical activities. These individuals see pieces and parts and can put the puzzle together without reading a book or an instruction manual. They thrive when they can actively engage with the material and manipulate objects or perform tasks; thus, they are very good at material handling, preparation, and various hands-on activities.

Besides knowing their passions, students need to find out if their passions align with their type of preferred learning. During Ryan's time with his students, he'll ask each one, "What do you want to be when you grow up?"

A student may say, "I want to be a professional athlete."

After getting to know the student (and his athletic abilities or lack of them), Ryan might respond something like this: "You want to be a professional football or baseball player? Well, it would be awesome if you could play football, but if for some reason that dream doesn't pan out, how about this—What if you could build a new stadium where they will play football? What if I could teach you how to become an ironworker, a boilermaker, a pipe fitter, or somebody who helps to build these huge sports complexes? How cool would that be?"

Our job as educators is to help young people identify what works for them and where in society they will have success.

In some families, parents may say their son is going to be a doctor or a lawyer, or even, "Our son's *got to* go to college to get a college degree," but they have no idea where they're going after they get to the college campus.

Or a student may say, "I really don't want to be an engineer, but I went into this field because my parents told me it was a great profession and because an engineer makes great money." This student may be more of a practical learner than a theoretical learner, and as a result, schooling might be very difficult for him. What if he started his professional pathway as a skilled tradesman instead?

Understanding first why engineering is so important is putting the horse in front of the cart, instead of the other way around. There isn't an engineer who gets the job done right initially; it takes somebody with a theoretical learning strength to listen to the practical person closely so the practical learner can teach them how to do their job with a deeper understanding of how the process of building and producing products works.

There are young men and women who go to college and get their engineering degree but don't have the practical ability and application to be elite engineers because they don't really know how things go together from a manufacturer's perspective. So, they're designing products, and the practical people who don't have the degree but are doing the building are replying to the engineer's designs, saying, "This can't be built like this." The theoretical designer doesn't have the practical experience and expertise to understand real-world application.

Engineers will tell the product producers that it 'should' work because it looks right on paper—and, therefore, it can be built. **If a person who is a theoretical learner can blend their strengths with practical learning and application as well, an ultimate engineer is born.** And if we had more of these ultimate engineers, our nation's infrastructures would go up quicker, faster, better, and easier.

As educators, parents, and mentors, the more we can help young people understand their strengths *and* learning preferences, the more likely they will be to succeed in a profession and as a human being so they can build a better community and a better family.

Ryan has a unique ability to find ways to make students not just good welders, fabricators, or engineers but universal learners and workers so those individuals can go on throughout life and build a better community and a better family. Like potting a new plant, he puts students (seeds) in the right soil so they can grow and prosper. In his class, he pours water and sunlight over them, **always nourishing his students to be a crop of hope for our community.**

To you young people who are looking for your niche and wondering where your skills and passions will fit in the world, be receptive to nourishment from those around you, those who can see things in you that you aren't aware of and who can help guide you to be the fullest and richest person to blossom in this beautiful world.

RYAN'S RULES:

1. Discover which type of learner you are, theoretical or practical.

2. Determine what your skills and passions are.

3. To grow and thrive, seek out and accept help in finding your best place in the world.

Applied knowledge + Changed behavior = Transformation

CHAPTER 20

The Touch

Ryan asked me one day, "How important is a handshake?"

I responded, "Well, I should be able to look you in the eyes and have a nice, firm grip that does not overpower but says I respect you as a person, and I cherish you as a brother."

That simple touch between two people is when it happens. That's when the bonds are formed with the energy that says you can do anything together, **an energy with which you can conquer the world because you are united in a shared mission.**

Ryan watches TikTok videos of football players and their coaches, and he gets emotional as he watches the amazing team chemistry. In one Ohio State TikTok, the coach embraced each player with fierce hugs and pats on the back when the players did something great. The vibration and energy that was flowing through those coaches to those individual players popped out of the phone. What stood out was the importance of the touch.

Once those players know that touch is there and that love and embrace is there, the energy ultimately consumes everyone—and that's how you become a very successful team. That positive aura is around everybody, not just one individual. When these individual teammates are embraced, they must feel the love. They must feel what they are doing is right, and as a result, they play as a team and play the game even harder because it's not just for themselves anymore.

There have been studies on the relationship between the frequency of high fives exchanged among teammates and the winning percentage of teams in various sports. The analysis of data from the study suggests that there is a significant positive correlation between high fives and winning. Therefore, the simple act of exchanging high fives positively impacts team performance.

Touching someone, whether with a high five or a pat on the back, reaffirms that you care for an individual and reinforces positive behavior.

TOUCH = FEELING VALUED

Embracing one another, whether it's a hug, handshake, or high five, is one thing society is much in need of because it is a way to create a relationship with non-verbal communication. For most individuals, the human touch is important to tell them they are loved and cared for with each passing day you are with them.

 **When someone feels valued, they are more likely to produce better results, whether in school, sports, their job, or at home.**

The 'touch' doesn't have to be a physical touch. For a teacher, when a student enters your classroom door, and you are not there to recognize them, they think that you don't even know they are there. If you can acknowledge them, even if it's across the classroom with "Hey, John, how you are doing today?", at least they know that you are recognizing them. That recognition is critical for their well-being.

So many of these kids come into a classroom, and they sit there and don't have any idea that anybody knows that they are there. If you recognize them when they come in, they're going to recognize you as they go out because they know that you care. Being a good and caring person simply requires a hello each morning and a goodbye when the class ends. **That little acknowledgment will create a lasting impression of the class and a memory of how you treated them.**

I have students who eat lunch in my classroom, and they get work done. I don't sit in the teacher's lounge. It's not that I don't like teachers (I love them; they're great people), but my mission is to serve, and I'm not going to sit down and relax as long as someone who is possibly going through the most difficult time in their life needs me. If you live in isolation, that's when the devil comes upon you, and you think that you're worthless. **When you are built up by others, by friendships and family and love, support, and caring, you feel like you're a superhero.**

HOW TIME BRINGS US TOGETHER

Think about your actions and the way you embrace another person—or do not embrace them. You are either building people up or diminishing them by not connecting with them on a personal level. That's why time is important for creating unity between people.

How many times per week do we sit down with our family and eat dinner together? Maybe once or twice a week if we're lucky. For many of us in the United States, our environment has changed so much that we don't have time for community at the dinner table. That's where community is. Consider making the decision to sit down more often for a meal with your family and friends. That intentional decision will strengthen a family or a friendship. **Time spent together cultivates a deeper relationship.** It's that simple.

Time, touch, and talking ultimately create a stronger community, and people want to be part of something where they feel loved, listened to, and supported.

There is nothing better than showing others how much you care. When you think about life, you've got to invest in the individuals you care about, and you've got to care about the individual they are coming to be. Every day, we choose to bring the energy and the power to others to uplift their ability to be great. Ryan says, **"I want my students to view me as an energy drink. I am their Monster, Red Bull, or Prime that fuels their fire to learn."**

The more we can take time and energy to bring our best, the more people will be attracted to that environment and be helped to transform into individuals who will hopefully reciprocate that energy into their families, their jobs, and their communities.

RYAN'S RULES:

1. Make a list of ways you can 'touch' and 'embrace' the team you want to strengthen and energize—your family, class, neighborhood, church—and then do at least one of those things each week.

2. Call, send a card, or have lunch with someone you care about but haven't seen for a while.

3. When you spend time with someone, put away the phone and talk to cultivate a deeper relationship.

Applied knowledge + Changed behavior = Transformation

CHAPTER 21

—

Mrs. Osmosis

A conversation between Ryan and a student in one of his classes at the community college:

Student: "I work at this place, and this old guy; all he does is yell."

Ryan: "Can I ask you a question?"

Student: "Sure."

 Ryan: "What type of individuals are you hanging out with when you're at your workplace?"

Student: "Well, I've got all these young buddies that I work with …"

Ryan: "There's your problem."

Student: "What's my problem?"

Ryan: "You're hanging out with the wrong people. Do you know why that old guy is always grumpy? Because **nobody's ever listening to him, and he's so sick of showing**

these kids how to do something and nobody's taking him seriously because they think they know everything. If you really want to learn, don't run away from the yelling, run toward the yelling, and try to help that man figure out why he is upset—because he is probably one of the smartest guys there."

Student: "You're probably right. He knows everything there. Nobody wants to work with him."

Ryan: "No one wants to be around him because you see him as a mean old man who yells all the time because things aren't done the right way. Another reason he may be upset is that he must constantly fix your projects to make them right. And could he have another reason to be grumpy each morning? How often are your buddies late?"

Student: "Oh, they're late every day."

Ryan: "How consistently are they showing up and putting forth a good effort each day?"

Student: "They'll do the work, but it takes them forever."

Ryan: "That's why you're listening to the wrong person. This guy's trying to teach you what he's learned from the last thirty years because he's on his way out of there, and he doesn't want what he has built there for thirty years to go away. The worst part of his frustration is, nobody's wanting to know his methodology of work and knowledge. Then one day, he will be gone, and you'll have no one to answer your questions, and you guys will be saying, 'Man, I wish he was still here.'

"Think about that. That's exactly what he wants. For you guys to learn from him. You know what you need to do? You need to go to that guy and say, 'Hey, can I get you a coffee?' Can you do something and show him that you are worthy of his time? Because, that guy, all he wants to do is show you what he knows because it's going to take you thirty years to learn what he knows.

"But guess what you're going to do? You're not going to put in the time or the effort to learn your craft to the best of your ability, and when you get stuck with something, you will just get somebody else to do it. But there won't be anybody else to do it because all the 'old guys' left after working thirty, forty, and sometimes fifty years in manufacturing. So, then what happens?"

Student: "What?"

Ryan: "The company collapses, and no jobs are available. To avoid that outcome, all you need to do is be nice to the 'old guys,' show up on time, listen to them, and learn from the most important educator in the world—who teaches everybody but never gets credit from anyone. Mrs. Osmosis.

"Who's Mrs. Osmosis? It is learning by watching. But

nobody is paying attention to her instructions. Nobody is paying attention to the skilled worker who is working right in front of them. Everyone's more worried about TikTok and Snapchat. They're worrying about how many people liked this post or that one. They're not paying attention to Mrs. Osmosis.

"Mrs. Osmosis can teach you how to build something by watching it happen. You can learn by watching her. You got to understand that Mrs. Osmosis is always working, and most of us are not paying attention. She is amongst us every second of every waking minute of every day.

"If we would just get our faces away from our screens, we would learn from watching people—good habits and bad; habits we want and those we don't want in our lives. When we are turning our heads the other way, we are denying education from Mrs. Osmosis.

"Nobody can teach us more than our own eyes. We need to focus our eyes on the wealth of knowledge in our community, where we have valuable access to someone who is a master in their field. (And yes, Mrs. Osmosis even works through YouTube videos.)

"The problem is that our eyes are distracted from good content by somebody jumping off a ledge into water or guzzling a bottle of soda and throwing up. These are the distractions that cause us to go into a black hole of uselessness and not take responsibility for our future and our children's future.

"So, don't run away from the person that is either yelling or talking loudly. They are trying to tell you, 'Listen, I'm trying to tell you what works, and this is how you get better and better at what you do and how you move up faster in a company and become better paid.' So, don't run away; run toward those 'old guys' and be a sponge to the years of experience and knowledge they have to offer.

"If we pay attention to all Mrs. Osmosis has to teach us and engage with somebody there, right in front of us in a real-life environment, with an actual physical touch, that's the most magical thing in the world. If you could just step back right now, think about this real-life scenario, and pivot to paying more attention to Mrs. Osmosis so you can soak up all the knowledge out there, you will be light-years ahead of the competition in your field.

"Pay attention to everything around you and sift through the good, the bad, and the ugly. Technology, relationships, and our culture are always evolving. Take note of how our society operates.

"If you want to be the cream of the crop for the future, then you must welcome Mrs. Osmosis in every area of your life so that you can have a joyful and healthier family, community, and country to live in."

RYAN'S RULES:

1. Be nice to the 'old guys.' Show up on time, listen to them, and learn from Mrs. Osmosis.

2. Pay more attention to the real life around you and less to the fake life on social media.

3. For one day each week, stay off social media and instead use the time to talk with someone whose character you respect and admire.

Applied knowledge + Changed behavior = Transformation

CHAPTER 22

One Shot

It is vital, truly vital, to be a good leader or representation of your family and your community by being able to communicate effectively and with authenticity. We get one shot in this life, so take responsibility and don't make excuses if your path isn't going the way you wanted it to go.

Instead, **be intentional with your thoughts, your actions, and your relationships.** These three areas are the trifecta for transforming into the person you were meant to be.

Having a disability does not define or restrict the outcome of your life. Ryan could have chosen the woe-is-me path and just worked an average job and paid the bills, but he didn't. He took the path of an outlier by learning differently and forging a path to reaching thousands of people in the welding and manufacturing field. He has helped to change cultures in companies by providing them with high-caliber welders and manufacturers who have high character as well. In some of these companies, 80 percent of their employees are Ryan's students, who have learned through

Mrs. Osmosis and have become what he has always wanted them to become, a 'savage' in the community. He defines a savage as someone who is not just going out there to be a welder but who also brings good knowledge to the job, is always willing to give 100 percent effort, has good community relationships, and keeps a good attitude.

Ryan speaks of goals beyond welding: "When we add oxygen to stagnant water, the oxygen brings the water back to life. If there's no oxygen in the water, there's no longer life in it, nothing living there. In the same way, we've got to add oxygen to our community, to our workplace, to our families, by adding our great-quality life as we show up, shut up, and do our jobs every day. And let me tell you, two of the most important crafts in the world are being a good mother and being a good father. By taking care of business at home, we build the best communities in the world."

We have one shot each day until the day we perish. With that mentality, the importance of everything and everyone is heightened in how we view our precious relationships, how we produce our work, and how we raise our children, whether they are under our roofs or not. The one shot may be that interaction with a student who just witnessed his mom pass out from drinking the night before or saw a brother get thrown in jail, arrested for breaking and entering. It may be one conversation with someone we rarely see but who has shown up at an inconvenient time. Our one shot may be a simple kindness to a stranger we'll never see again.

 **We don't know what people are going through, but how we show up each day to season and transform others' lives is what we can control.**

Ryan's experiences in life have provided the backbone of this book. He could have let his failures define him. He could have let more recent setbacks and changes in his life destroy the best version of who he is becoming each day, but he hasn't. Nor should you! **To stop growing and transforming into the people we were destined to be is a waste of the one shot we get.**

You may have noticed the formula at the end of each chapter:

Applied knowledge + Changed behavior = Transformation

If we can learn this, then we will truly learn how to live life—and not let life dictate our path. We'll become caring individuals who take responsibility and are resilient through all the trials and tribulations that will come up, and we'll gain wisdom to forge the path we have envisioned. Setbacks will come, and we must be ready to deal with them.

Our decisions each day impact our society. It is crucial to be a good citizen, son or daughter, mother or father. When you have character and do the right thing, the community prospers, the country is better off, and we all win, right? So, *everyone* out there, be responsible by being a great worker and modeling what your children, your peers, your neighbors, or your students need to see. That is how we live with the one-shot mentality.

Ryan has helped many organizations that he is passionate about, but everything in his life did not come about overnight. We must remember that all of us are capable of positively contributing to our culture and doing bigger and better things, but it takes growth, and growth takes time. Some people will reach a high-level position quickly; some will take longer; some will never move up the ladder of management or leadership. Ultimately, the 'position' doesn't matter; what matters most is the impact you make at home and in the community.

Ryan concludes, "If I surround myself with great people who will help me and work hard, I can accomplish almost anything. Just remember, you can't do it all, but you can do some great things in this life. That's how a household works. In a household, you have somebody who can cook and clean. You have somebody who can love. You have someone you can confide in. You have somebody who will earn the income. Sometimes it's one person; sometimes it's multiple people. Remember, it isn't one individual who runs the whole village. It's the whole community. And that's how we must look at society today. *Everybody* must contribute to having a great society, a great family, a great community, and a great nation."

We get one shot in life, so make it count by being a blessing to everyone around you because you may only have one time to make that lasting impression that could change the trajectory of a person's life—or possibly save one as well.

Epilogue

As we reflect upon the journey of Ryan, a dyslexic student who was once labeled as a "little dummy", he learned to adapt to his environment and rise to the top of his field. Through guidance, patience, and hard work, Ryan discovered his path to success, proving that learning differently does not hinder one's ability to achieve greatness.

As Ryan continues molding young minds, he sees a resemblance to his younger self in each student, reminding him of the importance of loving and caring for every individual. He is a Life changer, leaving an indelible impact on the lives of those whom he has taught and still teaches. With a clear vision, Ryan understands that action and passion are the driving forces for change. He has led by example, encouraging his students to step outside their comfort zones and shed their past. He has taught them to push past the fears that were holding them back, for memories are made through unique experiences and being around a nurturing and loving support system of people.

Ryan continues to instill in his students the habit of hard work pays off and that comparison is the thief of joy. He emphasized the significance of relationships and the role they play in one's life. He has also taught them that security blankets, which are family and friends, are essential elements to living a fulfilled life. Relationships are the glue that holds us stable and creates a joyful experience as we journey through life.

Ryan is also the master of using real-world examples to teach valuable lessons in welding and more importantly life. He teaches that failure is seen as an opportunity to learn and grow. Students who have worked with Ryan have also found fulfillment in their work, felt respected and loved, and know that he will always be there for them.

In the end, his students have felt valued and understand the importance of being intentional in all aspects of their lives. Ryan's legacy is lived through the lives he touched, and I am forever grateful for his guidance and support. I hope you enjoyed Molding Minds, and I pray that you unlock some of Ryan's Rules to live an exceptional and extraordinary life.

About the Authors

JOHN GRDINA AND RYAN EUBANK

JOHN GRDINA

John Grdina has spent nineteen years in education and leadership. He earned his bachelor's degree from John Carroll University, and a master's in education at Notre Dame College. He has also been a head baseball and golf coach for over a decade and continues to teach at Perry local schools, as a student success specialist. Currently, he is coaching cross country, basketball, and track for his children's school.

John is also the athletic director at Communion of Saints, a Catholic school on the east side of Cleveland. He is a life coach and has done over one hundred podcasts, has written 3 books, and is the owner of 40 Days of Deliverance; a 40-day program to improve your soul, body, and spirit. John is a father and has been married to his beautiful wife Megan, for over 16 years. John's mission in life is simple; to serve his family, community, and transform minds to live a legacy life.

He is a man of honor who has dedicated his life to helping others become the best versions of themselves. His brand, The John Grdina Classroom is a coaching platform that adds value to people's lives by focusing on areas that need to be transformed so everyone can live a more purposeful and fulfilled life. John is committed to personal growth, development, and self-improvement. He welcomes clients from all walks of life who are willing to put in the work to achieve their goals and transform their lives.

If you would like to contact John, below are the best places to reach him:

Website:

Email: grdinajohn@gmail.com

Phone: 440-941-4595

Facebook: John Grdina

Instagram: @jgrdina04

LinkedIn: John Grdina

TikTok: @jgrdina

RYAN EUBANK

Ryan Eubank has been a welding instructor for the past twenty-one years. He began his career at Lincoln Electric welding school and since then has taught at multiple career and technical schools on the east side of Cleveland, Ohio.

From Ryan's early years of education until the present, he has battled dyslexia and opinions that his learning disability would limit what he could do in life. Since high school, he has taken his learning disability and turned it from a negative to a positive, using his own experience with learning disabilities to become a game changer in the field of education, being a life coach and friend to his students.

Besides teaching high school students by day, Ryan is also an instructor at Lakeland Community College at night and on the weekends. He currently serves as the Chair of the Welding & Fabrication Technology Program and serves on local business panels. As co-owner and operator of Arc-hound, he employs former students and family. He is a subject matter expert in welding and an educational consultant to schools and colleges across the country.

Ryan has consistently and constantly served as a shepherd to so many in his family, community, country, and now the world. He does leadership training and teaches other instructors all over the world. He is also working with an organization called Project MFG to create national welding competitions that will attract and train young men and women in the trade.

Another project that he is working on is with an organization out of Tanzania. A new LNG plant is being built, and about 15,000 skilled trade laborers will be needed. The organization Ryan is working with is planning to build five welding schools, and he has been asked to help oversee the construction of the new welding facilities. It's about a five-year plan; they're starting to build the schools now so they will have skilled welders to fill the jobs at the new plant.

Ryan and his wife, Heather, have three beautiful children (Austin, Samantha, and Sarah). He hopes to continue teaching adults and students across America, creating strong discipline in the field of welding and helping to rebuild the educational system and strengthen our businesses with excellent workers.

Ryan loves his students, his life, his wife, and his family.

He's been blessed, and now he's paying it forward by taking walks with his students at 6:00 a.m., teaching them to become expert welders, helping the community by building or fixing equipment, working with business leaders, teaching pipe welding to international students, teaching other teachers how to bring hope and change to lives, and so much more. He wakes up each day excited to prove to the world that he is going to do great things for others and help our communities and ultimately our nation by producing the best people, welders, and future business owners.

If you would like to contact Ryan, below are the best places to reach him:

Email: reubank@weldunited.com

Phone: 440-796-9825

Acknowledgments

This book would not have been possible if it weren't for my family. I have the most profound respect for my parents (Tom and Susan), grandparents, wife (Megan), brothers (Todd and James), sister (Rachel), and children (Giuliana, Benjamin, Calvin, and Elijah). Solid families like the one I grew up in and that my wife and I have also established create an environment of hope, love, peace, and joy. Learning these daily behaviors as I grew up, along with being taught to respect and love my neighbor, developed my character. The foundation was laid for me, and I am blessed to have the opportunity now, in this book, to use my God-given talents to tell stories and offer lessons that will impact many lives.

Individuals besides my family who have helped me are Gail Michalski (former supervisor), Larry Logan (middle school history teacher), Bob Ritley (high school football coach), Mike Ryan (high school baseball coach), Jeff Hartmann (high school baseball coach), and many staff members at Perry, where I am currently employed.

I also want to thank all my coaches, teachers, priests, mentors, and groups of people with whom I've had relationships over the years, both in the past and in the present. Each person has helped to mold me into the person I have become. These influential people have allowed me to grow as an individual, and without this circle of motivating, humble, and loving people, this book may not have gotten into your hands today.

Dominic Ianiro helped with the first phase of editing this manuscript. Elaine Starner spent countless hours editing and making this book the finished product it is today. She truly is an expert in her craft, and along this journey, we forged a great friendship that will never be forgotten. Dominick Domasky, my publisher, challenged me to push my boundaries and think outside the box. His support and resourcefulness have helped me to keep motivating others through multiple platforms and experiences.

I also want to thank Ryan Eubank for his friendship and ability to overcome his fears, failures, and disability. He is a loyal friend who truly loves people and has worked extremely hard to make sure his family, friends, and students succeed in all aspects of their lives. I will forever be grateful for Ryan, all that he has taught me, for always believing in me and never leaving my side in this wild journey of life.

Lastly, but most importantly, the beloved Trinity (God, Jesus, and the Holy Spirit). Without the blessings given to me by the Triune God, none of this would have been possible.

Resources

THE POLAR BEAR PUZZLE:

Ryan brought this game to my school and played it with my baseball players to help me detect leadership in solving problems. It's also a good icebreaker. You can find other versions of it on the internet.

Playing this game will help you find out which kids have grit and patience. Some may get frustrated and even leave the group and want to have no part of it. You'll soon see which kids are going to push through hard problems and which are going to get frustrated and give up. From this, you'll also discover which students will probably need more support than the others. This may not be 100 percent accurate in all cases, but it will give you a clear indication of how students are going to tackle the game of content that you will be teaching.

All that is required for this activity is five dice and a place where students can be gathered around a table or desk and can see the results of the dice throw.

You might prepare your students with the following narrative and questions. Lead them to the answers if you must. The answers will give them clues to figuring out the puzzle.

1. Polar bears eat fish and seals. How do they catch fish and seals? (Through a hole in the ice.)

2. Polar bears always fish in pairs.

3. Wolves sometimes prey upon polar bear cubs. How do wolves travel? (In packs.)

They'll need to keep this information in mind as they figure out how to play this game.

Tell the group you belong to the Polar Bear Club, and anyone who figures out the secret of this puzzle can also be a member.

Now recite this poem:

Polar Bears, Polar Bears, gather round the ice hole
 In the days of Genghis Khan
 The game is in the name, the name is in the game

Roll any number of dice (usually five). Then ask, "How many polar bears, ice holes, and wolves do you see?"

Give them time to study the dice and try to figure out the answer. Then give them the correct answer and roll again, asking the same question on the next roll. "How many …?"

The key:

> *An ice hole: A dot in the center of the face of the dice. Thus, a 1, 3, or 5 would each have one ice hole.*
>
> *Polar Bears: Any pairs gathered 'around' the one dot in*

the center (bears around the ice hole). A 1 would be an ice hole with no bears. A 3 would have two bears. A 5 would have four bears.

Wolves: The 'pack' of six dots with no ice hole.

Keep a good pace and keep the energy flowing. Eventually, a student will figure out the patterns. Once he or she does, give them a big high five and tell them they are now part of the special Polar Bear Club.

Continue until at least half of the students know the answer.

HOW WELL DO YOU KNOW YOUR STUDENTS?

An activity that works well after the start of the school year was developed by Don Graves, a teacher who changed the way writing is taught and wrote professional books for educators. Do this activity several weeks into the school year and again toward the end of the year.

1. Create a three-columned chart on a piece of paper or on a simple table/spreadsheet on the computer.

2. In the left column, write your students' names in the order in which you remember them. (This alone is interesting. Who do you remember first? Who do you struggle to remember?)

3. In the middle column, write down one positive

thing about each student that doesn't have anything to do with schoolwork. (Jenny likes horses. Matt skateboards. Maria lives with her grandmother.)

4. In the third column, put a checkmark if you have talked with each student about this piece of knowledge. This helps us recognize how well we know our students, and—perhaps more importantly—how well they know we know them!

5. For students you struggled to remember, or for ones you didn't know as much about, make a commitment to connect with them in the next few days.

www.ingramcontent.com/pod-product-compliance
Lightning Source LLC
Chambersburg PA
CBHW021628120626
46545CB00002B/455